Gideon

Gideon

Power from Weakness

Jeff Lucas

Copyright © 2004 Jeff Lucas

First edition published by Kingsway

10 09 08 07 06 05 04   7 6 5 4 3 2 1

This revised and updated edition published in 2004 by
Spring Harvest Publishing Division and Authentic Media
9 Holdom Avenue, Bletchley, Milton Keynes, Bucks., MK1 1QR, UK
and P.O. Box 1047, Waynesboro, GA 30830-2047, USA
www.authenticmedia.co.uk

The right of Jeff Lucas to be
identified as the author of this work has been
asserted by him in accordance with the
Copyright, Designs and Patents Act 1988

British Library Cataloguing in Publication Data

A catalogue record for this book is available from the
British Library

ISBN 1-85078-557-0

Cover design by David Lund
Print Management by Adare Carwin
Printed and Bound in Denmark by Nørhaven Paperback

Dedication

Dedicated to the memory of Jory Glenn Pauls, born 1 August 1985, died 15 July 1998, dancing with God now.

Contents

'Gideon . . . who through faith conquered kingdoms . . .'
(Heb.11:32a, 33a)

The judges also with their respective names, those whose hearts did not fall into idolatry and who did not turn away from the Lord – may their memory be blessed!

May their bones revive from where they lie, and may the name of those who have been honoured live again in their sons!

Ben Sirach 46:11

INTRODUCTION

God doesn't call ready-made heroes when there's a bold job that needs to be done. He turns protesting, trembling people into brave souls: changed people who change the world.

Gideon was such a man: a reluctant, flawed hero. Our first sight of him is when Scripture draws back the curtain to reveal a frightened, nervous chap holed up in the now famous winepress. Pick up the camera of your imagination and take a snapshot of that scene. Gideon had heard countless fireside stories about the might and muscle of God, but these episodes of power were apparently locked up in the past. Even the greatest epics that celebrate the God of history don't ultimately satisfy us – we still need him to show up in the here and now. When he is absent, when the sands show no mark of his footprint and the winds carry no hint of his voice, then stories from the glory days taunt us rather than cheer us. Gideon was depressed.

Folk tradition had serenaded the Big God of yesterday, the God who had commanded the Red Sea to stand up for Gideon's forefathers – but the waves had long since fallen back, and the sea was flat and mirror calm now. Where had God gone?

Now, in the winepress, Gideon was in the tight, cold grip of hopelessness, as a seven-year-long national calamity rolled on without relief. He was a portrait of despair, a man with a head full of God-information but no sense of God-invasion. As I think of poor Gideon, his sweating back bent over as if bowed down by the futility of it all, I recall Annie Dillard's words in her novel *The Living*

> Hugh stood with stiff Lulu and supple Bert at the graveside. The Noonsacks stood together with their preacher. Before the funeral, in mourning for his father, they had shrieked and pounded on boards . . .
>
> At last big-faced Norval Tawes read Scripture and prayed, 'O Death, where is thy sting?' . . . and Hugh thought, *Just about everywhere, since you ask.*

Like Hugh, Gideon was haunted by a despair that seemed to mock the very existence of a caring God. Thus he was penned in, not just by granite winepress walls, but by thicker walls of hopelessness. Look at him there, and realise that he is not the first or last child of God to find themselves in the wrong spiritual and emotional geography. Remember the mighty Elijah, who felt the exhilarating wind of God in his hair on Mount Carmel, where fire snapped in a second out of the sky. Within days that same man who had summoned heaven's flames was hunched up, hermit-style, in a cave gouged into the side of Mount Sinai, the nation-shaking prophet who saw the Invisible Light now blinded by the thick gloom of his own fear and depression. Earthquake, wind and even a little more fire didn't budge the reluctant Elijah – it took an actual whisper from God to summon Elijah to step out, to break out to life and friendship and usefulness again. Both Elijah and Gideon had found themselves not only in a cave and a winepress in physical terms, but also in mental prisons, strongholds if you will.

Scripture makes it clear that the enemy, Satan – Gideon's enemy, Elijah's enemy and ours too – is a masterful architect and builder of caves and winepresses. He is eager to build mental and emotional caves where we can live out our days, unhappily ever after. These strongholds are 'houses of thoughts' where we sit and languish and occasionally dream of the vague possibility that God might rise up and help us, but in the meantime we crouch low in the darkness. And there are so many prisons available. Many Christians seem to have a pristine morality, and an orthodox theology, but still live an existence of quiet despair; the good news has not been so good for them and, in a way, their belief in the 'abundant life' only serves to mock them in their captivity. I know that feeling well. I have identified a number of areas where I know I need to step out from the emotional and spiritual winepresses where I have slumped fearfully for too many days. Freedom begins with truth, so why not take a few minutes now to read through Judges 6, 7 and 8. An overview of the story will be invaluable as you journey with me back to Gideon's world.

One word of explanation. Some readers might find themselves fidgeting uncomfortably as I use a little imagination in revisiting Gideon's story. Very shortly I will describe an attack scene which is not a specific biblical episode. What the Bible does tell us is that there were attacks; the historical detail comes from my research, the narrative from my imagination. So, in dipping into the ink of creativity in an attempt to make the story 'live', am I guilty of 'adding to Scripture'?

As this book unfolds, you will discover biblical exegesis, hopefully creative narrative and prose, as well as personal illustrations from my own experience. I offer the mixture without apology, but permit me a word of explanation. First, let me assure you that I have tried to allow my imagination to run only along lines that are consistent with both the biblical text and historical authenticity. So, when I describe Gideon's house in Chapter 2, I do so not because the *Bible* describes his home, but as a result of extensive historical research into housing construction in that period.

Secondly, I am encouraged by the teaching method called *Midrashim*, which the rabbis have used since time immemorial. 'Midrashim' means 'to go in search of' and 'to inquire'. The rabbis of old would examine the biblical stories, seek to discover the meaning of those episodes for their own lives and times and sometimes develop other stories in order to 'fill in the gaps' for the sake of illustration and application. These story collections were then handed down in the form of popular folk tradition, and were used in sermons preached in the synagogues. In 'filling in the gaps' the rabbis demonstrated that they were gifted with fertile imaginations as well as a profound understanding of the nature of God and his creation. They would construct contemporary analogies, taking the old stories in hand and then saying, 'Let me put it this way', thus making the old new. Of course the Lord Jesus used the tool of analogy with great effect in his colourful and parabolic teaching style. Storytelling has long held a central place in Jewish tradition. This distinctly Jewish method of biblical interpretation has motivated me to imagine, to dig, to dream and then shamelessly to jump back and forth between Gideon's world and our own. This is Midrashim: yesterday's stories speaking to today.

So, at times, you may well disagree with my interpretation of the story. Be released and free so to do!

Midrashim did not insist that one interpretation of Scripture alone be declared as correct. As one lover of Midrashim has observed, 'For any given passage of Scripture, several stories or interpretations of various rabbis are presented side by side in collections of Midrashim. Those who collected these stories saw no reason to decide which one was the right interpretation . . .'[1]

As you come with me to Gideon's world, perhaps you will nod in agreement at times and violently shake your head in passionate disagreement at others. That's fine. Just allow the Lord to make the application of the story relevant and poignant for where *you* live.

The prophetic theme that I want to investigate is simple: Gideon was holed up, God broke in and Gideon broke out, at least for a while. Let's allow the Lord to help us follow Gideon out of our gloomy, musty winepresses, out into the bright sunshine and fresh air of freedom.

Jeff Lucas

---

[1] Michael E. Williams, *The Storytellers' Companion to the Bible*, Vol. 3 (Abingdon Press, 1993), pp. 17–19

Chapter One

In Trouble in the Promised Land

> Again the Israelites did evil in the eyes of the LORD, and
> for seven years he gave them into the hands of the
> Midianites. (Judg. 6:1)

It was good to hear the delicious sound of laughter
again.

Hands on hips, the woman arched her aching back,
ran the palm of a calloused hand across her damp brow
and surveyed the busy scene around her. The wheat
bowed and swayed gently in a warm sirocco wind and
harvest workers hurried and chattered between the
golden ripe waves. The woman could not hear
the details of their distant conversations, but their easy
laughter said it all. Hopes were high. A bumper crop
could bring a hundredfold return. Shielding her eyes
against the flaming sun, she could just make out their
smiles. The crops had survived the threat of hail, mildew
and the unreliability of the April rains – 'the latter rains',
as they were known. Harvest time was a season to smile.
She enjoyed the luxurious swishing sound of a hundred
bronze sickles sweeping through the thick waves. The
rhythmic melody of harvest work, the sound that meant

food in the children's bellies through the winter, was music to the ear.

Was it just her imagination, or was there a vague sense of anxiety in the air? Everybody seemed to be working just a little faster today. The reapers swept their sickles quickly, urgently across the proud wheat, shearing it high on the stalk. Others stepped forward immediately to gather the newly shorn ears of corn into sheaves. The sheaves would then be heaped together, ready for transportation. In peacetime, great ox carts with huge, eight-spoked wheels would trundle the grain to the village threshing floor. So why the sense of hurry and the hint of urgent nervousness in their laughter now? Had they heard a rumour of yet another raid?

She scanned the lilting field again. It was teeming with workers. She'd heard stories about the ancient custom of leaving the corners of fields unharvested, so that the poor, the aliens and the destitute could benefit from the leftovers. Evidently Yahweh had commanded this practice in his Law. Sometimes the gleaners would trail through the fields, following up after the reapers, scrabbling for their leftovers. But these were more modern, enlightened times. Yahweh was just one of a variety of gods on offer, so some of the farmers didn't bother any more. The workers hurried greedily to every square cubit of field. She peered through the shimmering heat haze in search of her sons. They were down there somewhere, their strong, red-browned shoulders firmed by ten thousand sweeps of the sickle, boys in men's bodies. Where were they, those men of hers?

Then she saw them both, and was immediately puzzled. Her youngest had suddenly stopped working, the sickle hanging limp at his side. He was gazing intently at the eastern horizon. Some of the other reapers jabbed their fingers at something in the distance, their voices urgent, louder now, agitation stark on their faces. Desperately, the woman searched the landscape, finding nothing with her eyes, but her sinking heart seeing the inevitable. She knew what was out there. They all knew. During the long months of peace, they had tried to convince themselves that the raiders had changed their six-year strategy, that the deadly skirmishes were finished. Night after night they had toasted the end of the Midianite attacks with too many cups of spiced date wine. Surely the nightmare was over – the gang rapes, the arbitrary killings and the pillaging of their crops – surely it was ended. Perhaps it was a confidence birthed by a heady cocktail of herbs and alcohol, but they had dared to hope again. They had even ventured a joke or two about the dark men who stomped across the land on camels, hoping perhaps that the drunken mirth would drive the lingering fear from their souls. The Midianites had been the first warriors in history to tame the camel and use it as a battle steed. What fearsome, ugly monsters they were – word had it that the bite of the camel nearly always tore a fatal, festering wound. Perhaps the gods had visited the cursed animals with a plague. Now they could live in peace and prosperity again: the Promised Land would be the land of promise once more. They drank another cup, a hopeful toast to better days. But deep down inside, they all knew the truth: the Midianites were just biding their time, waiting patiently, letting the Hebrew farmers do all the hard work, until harvest time. And then they would crowd the horizon yet again, their yellowing teeth clenched in hatred, eyes narrowed with lust. They came to kill, to maim, to take, just as they did every year. But most of all, they came as strutting warriors to humiliate the cowering Hebrews.

The woman felt them beneath her feet before she saw them. It was like an earthquake, a growing, irresistible turmoil deep in the soil. And then the ground beneath her feet began to reverberate, the final confirmation of their coming.

There it was, a faraway cloud of dust billowing up to stain the clear afternoon sky. Fear formed a scream in the woman's throat. She turned and began to run westward, a useless attempt to escape the dust cloud and the raiders it announced. And then she remembered her sons, boys in men's bodies.

❋   ❋   ❋   ❋

Two miles away, the Bedouin chieftain threw back his head of filthy, tangled black hair and howled a demonic battle oath. No one heard it, such was the deafening roar of camel hooves pounding across the plain. The fearsome, angular beasts scooped up great clouds of sand as they leapt and lurched their clumsy way forward. The chieftain laughed again, his ink-black eyes focused on the fleeing Hebrews, frantically scattering, scurrying away like desert ants suddenly disturbed. What a sight to behold! He was a man fully alive now, hot blood speeding through his veins, delirious with an intoxicating mixture of power, greed and lust. Time to savour the moment. He raised his arm quickly and within seconds all his men had brought their camels to a halt, steam rising quickly from their coarse, stinking frames. They all waited in sudden silence, save the sound of the animals' impatient snorting and stomping. The chief peered again through the dust at the still distant Hebrews, terrified cowards who now chose to spend the last few minutes of life doing what the Hebrews did best; running. He looked around at his men, eager to share the sight with his brothers, enjoying the mad blaze of victory in their eyes. These were the *Bene Qedem*, the

'Children of the East'. A fierce nomadic tribe, their home was the northern Syrian desert. The chief looked off to their left flank, where the band of warriors known as the 'Terror of Midian' were also at a halt. Infamous for their love of unspeakable sexual perversity – they had literally made a religion out of their putrid desires – the Midianites were long-time arch-enemies of Israel. Hundreds of years earlier, Joseph's jealous brothers had conspired together and sold him for twenty shekels to some passing Midianite merchants (Gen. 37:28). In later history Moses had married a Midianite woman, Zipporah, and had taken counsel from her father, Jethro, a Midianite priest (Ex. 18:24). But the Hebrews had always regarded the Midianites as a pollutant, a people of corruption. Moses himself had led a terrible attack on the Midianite city kings – Evi, Rekem, Zur, Hur and Reba (Num. 31:8). He had burned their cities and camps to the ground and had ordered the massacre of all the men, boys and even women – only the virgins were spared, some thirty-two thousand of them. A bitter hatred for the Hebrews had raged throughout Midianite history. Vengeance was sweet.

Then, off to the right flank, the Amalekites drew their camels to a halt. They too were historic arch-enemies of Israel. Many years earlier Israel had been baptised in the art of battle in a bloody encounter with the Amalekites (Ex. 17:8). Joshua, their ancient hero, had led a great slaughter that day. The valley of Rephidim had run red with Amalek blood. Moses had put an eternal curse on the Amalekites in the name of his God. The cursed took every opportunity to take revenge. Within seconds, Moses' descendants would be begging, crying out for the mercy of a swift death.

The warriors looked eagerly for the command to advance, for the blood-letting to begin, but the chieftain was in no hurry. Let the Hebrews run for a few more moments – better sport for the hunt. These raids were almost too easy. There was a time, not so very long ago, when the Hebrews had been a force to be reckoned with. They had not always been the cowering fugitives that were scattering before him. As a young man, he remembered how fear tore at his heart as he heard the campfire stories. He could almost recite them word for word, the tales of terrible enemies from the past and old blood spilled without mercy. For seventy-five long years the Hebrews had known strong, fine leadership, as *shofets* or 'judges' arose among them. Awesome fighters, these men – and women – had gained respect, even from sworn enemies. Men like Othniel, a name from a hundred years ago. A fearful tyrant city king by the name of Cushranrishathaim ('Cushan of double wickedness') had successfully raided from northern Syria and had managed to enslave numbers of the Hebrews for eight years. And then the legendary Othniel ('the powerful one') had repelled this dark invader, bringing years of peace for the Israeli settlers. Other Hebrew names had become legends in the land, such as Ehud the strong, the famous left-handed man with the double-edged sword, a man with a huge heart and laughter in his soul. Generations had roared when they heard of how Ehud announced that he had a divine message for fat King Eglon. He stuck a sword so deep into Eglon's huge belly that the sword came straight through, out of his back, and then all that fat closed over the hilt. Ehud had made his getaway while the king's guards convinced themselves that the king was engaged in the important business of a bowel movement, so should not be disturbed. What a man!

There had been other worthy opponents in Hebrew history, like Shamgar the city king of Bethanath in

Galilee. Word had it that he had attacked the Philistines, guardians of sophisticated and developed weaponry, and had wiped out six hundred of them – with an ox goad as his secret weapon!

Then there were names that even the *Qedem* feared: Judge Deborah, the wild woman from Ephraim, and her colleague Barak, who just twenty-five years earlier had led the Hebrews to the great victory on the Kishori River. Jabin, a Canaanite city king, had terrorised the Hebrews for around twenty years. He had a large army ably led by one General Sisera, who was not only a renowned warrior, but also commanded a huge army and boasted nine hundred chariots of iron. The Hebrews were terrified of Sisera – their teachers said that his shout could demolish a city's walls and freeze the wildest of beasts in fear. It was said that it took nine hundred horses to pull his mighty chariot and that when he went swimming, the fish that got trapped in his beard would feed a host of famished hunters. He was said to have conquered the whole known world by the time he was thirty years old. Weary of the years of oppression and convinced that her God would help her, Deborah commanded Barak to lead an army of just ten thousand troops into battle against Sisera. Barak agreed, but insisted that Deborah accompany the troops as they went to war. During the terrible fighting, a thunderstorm broke out, the Kishon flooded the whole area, the infamous chariots were mud-bound and useless, and Israel triumphed, putting Jabin's entire army to the sword in a single day. Even General Sisera was not spared. Escaping from the battlefield, he thought that he could find sanctuary and rest in the tent of Jael, a Kenite woman. She gave him goat's milk and wine, covered him with a blanket, placed fresh fragrant roses all around him and promised to stand guard while he slept.

As he drifted into sleep, she swung a heavy mallet high and drove a tent peg right through his head.

The chieftain spat on the ground, his face creased with contempt. There had been a time when the Hebrews were worth fighting. But those days were gone for ever. Now there was no challenge. They were just maggots, worthy only to be burned. So burn them now, let them blacken in the fire and writhe and wriggle and die in long-deserved agony . . .

He raised his arm again. They had delayed enough. With a vicious kick to his huge, clumsy steed, he waved his men forward again, anxious now to reach the fields and to find the women.

❈   ❈   ❈   ❈

How can you be in trouble in a promised land? It's easy. Just emigrate to that land and, once you're there, gradually forget the God of promise who led you there in the first place. Some 3,100 years ago, Israel had taken partial possession of that prized land which had eluded their wilderness-wandering ancestors, but there wasn't much proverbial fat for them to live on, or milk and honey for that matter. They had finally arrived at the strip of land called Canaan, one hundred and eighty miles long and just forty miles wide. Spiritual amnesia, a creeping national epidemic, had quickly begun to set in.

Joshua's marauding pioneers who had swept across the Jordan as conquering invaders were all long buried. Now, around a century and a half later, Israel was a generation that had never known for themselves the widening eyes and stunned gasps that come when God parts a river or a sea so you can cross in safety. They didn't know how to dance the celebration jig that begins when Pharaoh's mighty chariots slide for ever beneath the waves – those who could teach them the steps had long since turned to dust. They had heard that magical story of the city of Jericho, but didn't know for themselves the sense of awe that floods your soul when you shout at a fortified wall and watch it collapse on command. The fighting faith had died with their great-great-grand-parents. Now the people of Israel were tame, benign settlers, impotent fugitives. The victors had become victims. How could this be?

For a start, Israel was facing a major military challenge because of earlier compromises. Ironically, Egypt, its old oppressor three hundred miles south, was no longer a serious threat. The mighty empire of the Pharaohs was crumbling now, exhausted from repeated battles with rebellious vassals like the Philistines, the 'people of the sea'. The Egyptian economy was withered by the perpetual war effort and further drained by her tax-exempt pagan temples. Law and order was breaking down and even the royal tombs were being looted. The sun was finally setting on the Pharaohs.

Israel's problem was much closer to home: they had never fully occupied the land of Canaan as God commanded. This was not a land of chaotic, scattered nomads. Some cities had been settled by a variety of Semitic tribes for over two thousand years prior to the arrival of the Hebrew invaders. Although Canaan was not blessed with an abundance of natural resources, it was strategically placed geographically, and so for years the superpowers of history had used it either as a buffer state for military protection, or as an ideal advance base for wider campaigns of expansion. General Joshua had taken the pathway of least resistance when he led the conquest, and consequently many cities were still held in the hands of Canaanite *meleks*, or city kings. The Canaanites had been vassals of Egypt, but the cities increasingly became independent mini-states with their own economies, particularly as the distant Egyptians weakened. There was constant bickering between these city states, which the Egyptians had happily tolerated. In fact, the continuous feuding prevented the development of a powerful Canaanite coalition and had ensured a steady flow of tax money into the Egyptian coffers. Other cities like Gezer and Jerusalem remained outside of lasting Hebrew control for hundreds of years and would not be conclusively taken until the time of David's reign – a city taken in one skirmish did not mean that the city was finally conquered. It could easily be lost in the next battle. And then, to further complicate matters, the south-west coast was the site of five Philistine garrison cities – Gaza, Ashkelon, Ashdod, Ekron and Gath – each ruled by a *seren* or tyrant king. As with the Canaanites, these cities had originally been established as outposts for the Egyptian Pharaohs, but now, as that empire was in its death throes, the Philistines were establishing their own independence and flexing their muscles – they also held a number of strategic cities on the Plain of Esdraelon and on into the Jordan Valley. Canaan was a melting pot of nomadic tribes, rival clans and city states. Israel found military success in the hill country, as they were accomplished infantry who fought well on foot. But they were out of their league on the plains, where the chariots of the Canaanites and the Philistines ruled supreme. The Canaanites had a firm monopoly on iron production and managed to keep their production technique a closely guarded industrial secret until David's time (Josh. 17:16; Judg. 1:19). Thus Israel had no chariots at this stage, and had not developed the sophisticated weaponry of their enemies, such as the strong compound Asiatic bow.

The Israelites initially adapted to their limitations with ingenuity and skilful engineering, which is surprising as generally their efforts at building were vastly inferior to those of the Canaanites. But here they did well, constructing lime-lined plaster cisterns for water supplies – some of which survive today – enabling them to develop new towns in previously inhospitable locations. They also cleared the forests that had covered much of the highlands east and west of the Jordan, which made excellent land for cultivation. But the geographical scattering of the tribes still posed a constant threat to their sense of national identity. The book of Judges describes an Israel with a clear and invaluable sense of nationhood, using the term 'Israel' more than any other book of the Hebrew Bible. The armies are known as 'the men of Israel'. God is seen as dealing with the nation as a whole, judging *Israel*, testing *Israel*. The book also uses terms like 'the camp of Israel' and 'the misery of Israel'. Despite ongoing rivalry and banter between the tribes, a national call to arms was a summons that every tribe was expected to respond to, or risk a serious curse (Judg. 5:15-17,23). But Israel was still a nation beset with division. There was no central government to provide cohesion. Each tribe was led by elders (*zeqenim*) who carried out local executive functions, sitting at the city gates and resolving civil and judicial disputes. We assume that those leaders would come together to resolve issues of national importance – Judges contains examples of such gatherings – but there was no capital city and no national administrative machinery in place.

So what was it that gave these scattered tribes their sense of national identity? How did Israel survive as a nation throughout two hundred years of hard struggle between the conquest and the development of the monarchy?

I believe that the answer is to be found as we consider her corporate faith. Israel was held together by a unique religion, which was not centred around abstract and vague doctrines about God. They were the people who owed their very birth and ongoing existence to the dynamic intervention of the one God; Yahweh. He had danced into their history as Rescuer and Redeemer and made them a *chosen* people in a *promised* land. The glorious twin stories of yesteryear, Exodus and Sinai, were both pivotal events that lingered in the Hebrew psyche and even through their years of backsliding, the people called Israel held a haunting sense of destiny in their hearts. As they remembered the obedient Red Sea standing up impossibly at Moses' command, and the trembling mountain where the Law was given, they recalled more than dusty history. They were who they were because of those epic happenings. John Bright comments

> We can find no period in Israel's history when she did not believe she was the chosen people of Yahweh . . . the prophets and the . . . writers continually hark back to the exodus as the unforgettable example of the power and grace of Yahweh calling a people to himself . . . it is clear that from earliest times Israel saw herself as a people chosen by Yahweh, and the object of his special favour.[2]

This sense of being chosen transcended sentimentality – they were now bound by a covenant agreement with God. They were members of a dynamic, radical new society, not based in blood but under the election and rule of God, the Old Testament kingdom of God. Having said this, they rarely used the title 'king' to refer to

---

[2] John Bright, *A History of Israel* (SCM Press, 1960), pp. 144–145

Yahweh. Bearing in mind that most kings were only in charge of cities, and thus were petty kings, it was felt that king was too lowly a designation for God. Nonetheless, the ark was seen as Yahweh's throne (Num. 10:33 ff.), and Israel's earliest poets hailed him as king (Ex. 15:7; Ps. 29:10). He was the rescuing ruler of Israel, delivering them by his *hesed* (his gracious act, Ex. 15:1-18) and so now they were a nation that belonged to God (Num. 23:9), and enjoyed his protection (Ps. 68:19 ff.). This knowledge brought no sense of superiority or vain pride. They knew that all of this was due only to the lavish undeserved favour of Yahweh.

Yahweh was the dynamic, travelling king as well. Pagan religion held no long-term hope for the future, no plan of things. Pagan rituals were about persuading the gods by magic incantation to give you a good crop this year – manipulation for the sake of the immediate. 'The ancient paganisms lacked any sense of a divine guidance of history towards a goal.'[3]

Israel, however, had a clear expectation of blessing and prosperity at the hands of their God. He was going somewhere. Hadn't he called them from the oppressive status quo of Egyptian bondage to a bright new future in a faraway place called Canaan? Israel's God was not some static being to be magically appeased, rather he was at the head of his people, leading them forward in triumph if they would follow him. Even the ark of the covenant was kept in a tent as a living reminder of the God who, to quote one author, was committed to 'tenting it with his people'. Towards the end of the Judges period, the ark was placed in a permanent structure, but the feeling remained that the proper housing for the throne of Yahweh was a tent. Israel's God was no

---

[3] John Bright, *A History of Israel*

mere local nature deity. Rather, he was the Creator of the cosmos, the *yahweh asher yihweh* ('he who causes to be what comes into existence'). This lofty God demanded unconditional loyalty from his subjects, prohibiting them from worshipping other gods (Ex. 22:20; 34:14). He needed no consort – Hebrew has no word for goddess. The Hebrews believed that Yahweh was surrounded by a royal court of angels, but unlike their pagan neighbours, these beings were never to be worshipped (Deut. 4:19). It wasn't so much that Israel denied the existence of other gods, they just refused them the status of godship, and therefore 'undeified' those beings. They were called to worship without images, which was again in stark contrast to their neighbours. The second commandment made this clear, and indeed archaeology has never uncovered an image of Yahweh.

The shrine where the ark was kept was probably the focus of religious life. Most believe that during the period of the Judges the ark was mainly kept at Shiloh. It was here that the tribal chiefs – the *nasi* – would gather. Although localised shrines existed, the heart of Israel's corporate life was the shrine, where it is thought that great annual feasts would provide a gathering point for the clans. Some historians suggest that once a year all of Israel would gather (Judg. 21:19) for the autumn feast of ingathering.

So Israel was Israel because of her covenant with Yahweh. But now she was in mortal danger. That sacred agreement was being systematically violated. A satanic courtship with Canaanite religion was underway, a partnership truly spawned in hell. Considering Israel's unique experience of the living God, we might wonder how they could be consistently seduced into meaningless occult activity. Certainly they had been repeatedly warned about the evils of mingling their religion with that of the local inhabitants. So why did they fall, time and time again, into the same obvious snares? I believe that there are two reasons: similarity and sex.

Canaanite religion was similar in some respects to the religion of Israel. Offerings of sheep and cattle were given in worship; a priesthood existed, with a high priest taking charge of twelve priestly families. The Canaanites also had priest scribes to care for their sacred writings. Like Israel, their festivals were based around the farming year, as one would expect in this agricultural culture. They had psalmists who would sing liturgies in their ceremonies. There were prophets who would speak on behalf of their gods. And they even had a god of covenant, Baal Berith – the lord of the covenant – who was worshipped at Shechem. The problem of similarity was further compounded by the fact that the Canaanite Baal was a bull, as was Amon-Re, the Egyptian god, and Asshur, the Assyrian god. Culturally, the idea of a bull as an object of worship was very strong. Thus Israel became easily drawn into bull worship, most obviously as they worshipped the golden calf in the Sinai wilderness (Ex. 32). Hosea would lament with sarcasm, 'Men kiss calves!' (Hos. 13:2). Baal was described as the Rider of the Clouds, who sits on a heavenly throne and hurls down thunderbolts, and Yahweh is described in exactly the same terms (Ps. 2:4; 18:13; 77:18; 103:19; 144:6). Israel's affections were harnessed by the subtle wooing that comes when you are surrounded by so-called 'similar' religion: 'This isn't so different from our way, is it?'

But if there was subtlety in the similarities, then there was a driving force in the temptation to sexual abandon. Stray hormones have been the downfall of humanity from the beginning, and Canaanite religion was a consumer-driven, take-your-pick cult where you could worship and explore the darker side of your sexuality at the same time. A large number of gods were available to worship, and the worshipper could pay homage either at a simple stone altar or in elaborate temples built for the purpose. The Canaanites believed that the great god El was in charge. He was a rather shadowy figure, preferring to stay in the background, working through other gods that he spawned. El, it was believed, had fathered seventy other deities as a result of his relationship with the goddess Asherah, 'the Mistress of the Sea, the Creatress of the gods'. Asherah poles, trees with the limbs lopped off, stood guard at Canaanite shrines. Baal was 'the prime minister' of the gods, but he only derived his authority from El himself. He had a mistress too – Anat, goddess of war, a particularly violent deity who was often portrayed as being up to her hips with the blood, heads and hands of her enemies. A fragment of a Baal epic says of Anat

> She smites the people of the seashore
> Destroys mankind of the sunrise
> She piles up heads on her back
> She ties up hands in her bundle
> Anat gluts her liver with laughter
> Her heart is filled with joy.[4]

Other texts describe Anat riding naked astride a galloping horse, waving weapons of battle. The Canaanites often consecrated a new building by burying children alive in the foundations – they were placed in jars and buried at the corners of the house or just under the door jambs. The skeleton of a fifteen-year-old girl buried alive

---

[4] C. H. Gordon, *Ugaritic Literature: A Comprehensive Translation of the Poetic and Prose Texts* (Rome: Pontifical Biblical Institute, 1949)

in this manner has been discovered in the ruins of a fortress at Megiddo. When a society worships bloodshed, it sheds blood easily and without conscience.

Anat was also the goddess of sex and passion. Obscene carvings have been recovered from Ras Shamra depicting her in lewd contortions. Other female deities were similarly portrayed with hugely exaggerated sexual organs. The Canaanites believed that this sex and violence icon was the queen of heaven and so naturally this sanctioned the use of male and female temple prostitutes. Cult objects included lilies (sex appeal) and serpents (fertility). Sexual corruption was considered holy. Anat, as a goddess/sacred prostitute, was known as *qudshu* ('the holy one'). Holiness for the Canaanites referred to anything dedicated to the service of a deity. It was thus a holiness devoid of integrity or morality, nothing more than pornographic magic. And so the religion of the Canaanites offered a tantalising and tempting mingling of spirituality and sensuality to the Israelites, and throughout their history they struggled with a tendency to stray into that so-called spirituality. Elijah's later showdown with the prophets of Baal is testimony to the tenacity of this evil. Baal is the most mentioned of the Canaanite gods. Temples were built in his honour. He was known chiefly as the god of fertility and the god of the storm, and so it was very important for the farmers to keep Baal happy and appeased! And then there was Resheph, god of pestilence, and Mot, the god of drought and death.

Israel's real long-term and primary enemy was not the camel-riding Midianites or the persistent Amalekites. She herself was her own worst enemy. Her real problem was not political or military – these were but symptoms of a deeper cancer. Even the mighty chariots of Sisera had been overthrown when Israel was right with her God. Had not Deborah proved that? The psalmist sums it up beautifully: 'Some trust in chariots and some in horses, but we trust in the name of the LORD our God' (Ps. 20:7).

The early chapters of Judges testify to the fact that the people of Israel could conquer when the Lord was with them (Judg. 1:19). But now they had God as their enemy: 'the LORD gave them into the hands of the Midianites . . . for seven years' (Judg. 6:1). The lover had become judge. '. . . The hand of the LORD was against them to defeat them' (Judg. 2:15). Terry Virgo explains it concisely

> In reading the Old Testament we find that God often strengthens Israel's pagan enemies when Israel turned away from him – a fact that bewildered Habakkuk and a truth that Jeremiah had to live with throughout his entire ministry.[5]

Israel was reaping the seeds of rebellion and unfaithfulness that had been sown throughout decades of treachery. It has been said that it took a miracle to get Israel out of Egypt, but God never quite got Egypt out of Israel. History repeatedly testified to that tragic truth. Israel seemed hell-bent on walking a depressing cycle, like their ancestors long before who wandered in wilderness circles for forty long years. This was a new generation, but on a familiar trek still. Rebellion. Retribution. Repentance. Rescue. Rebellion. Retribution . . .

The cycle had included brighter moments when God raised up judges in answer to the people's cry for help, as we have already seen. These charismatic women and men bore no resemblance to the austere, costumed indi-

---

[5] Terry Virgo, *Men of Destiny* (Eastbourne: Kingsway, 1997)

viduals who preside over our modern courtrooms. They
settled disputes in peace-time (Judg. 4:5; 1 Sam. 7:15-17)
– like Deborah, who set up court under her favourite
tree – but then were the instrument of Yahweh to lead
the people into holy war in times of threat. They were
the *shofets* ('judges') and the *mosia* ('deliverers'). These
judges were Yahweh's own idea – he raised them up
(Judg. 2:16,18), called them (Judg. 6:11–40), stirred them
(Judg. 13:25) and planned their strategy (Judg. 7:2–23).
The Spirit of God 'rushed' upon the judges (Judg.3:10;
11:29; 14:6,19; 15:14) and clothed them (Judg. 6:34).
Outside of the Spirit of Yahweh, they had no power to
act (Judg. 16:20). Some of them were rascals like
Jephthah, who has been described as nothing more than
a bandit who knew how to strike a good deal. There was
Samson, a man of incredible muscle with a besetting
appetite for bawdy pranks and fast women. They were
not so much qualified to act, but were authorised by
God to do so. The judges enjoyed enormous prestige,
but were no kings – they were the representatives of the
God-King. They were not reformers in any sense. None
of them was charged by Yahweh to launch a crusade
against idolatry or to call the people back to the true God
(only Samuel did this and he did so as a prophet rather
than a judge).

Rather, the primary function of the judge was to relieve
military pressure from foreign nations, nations that
Yahweh was himself using as instruments of judgement.
But now, twenty-five years had passed since Deborah's
prophetic song and the celebrated victory that followed.
The Hebrews had been forced to abandon their towns
and flee to cave strongholds in the hills; the situation was
desperate. Was there any word from the Lord?

❀   ❀   ❀   ❀

The old man drew his tired body up to full height and waited. He looked around at the gathering crowd and immediately struggled to hold back a torrent of tears. It was the look in their eyes that broke his heart. Empty. Lifeless. Cold. Light and joy chased away by the cruel, harsh years. The older ones, weary beyond belief and just ready, resigned for death. The younger ones, who had never known anything else except this fear and hiding, had never lived any other way. Oh, how have you come to this, my lovely, dancing princess Israel? The lengthening shadows were gathering fast now, and soon the humble village would be settling in for another night. But no feast to end this day. No great flames to chase the darkness away and warm their chilled souls. A big fire at harvest time was too dangerous, an invitation for miles to the raiders in the dark.

The people settled to silence. Word was that the old man had had a dream in the night and that Yahweh had spoken to him. There were one or two who remembered Deborah's dream of years ago, a dream that stirred a nation, a dream that broke Israel out of her sin-sleep and caused her to sing again, at least for a while. Could they dare to begin to hope for another such dream now? Would there be another with the spirit of Barak; another great call to arms, with the promise of a mighty victory again; one last glory day? How wonderful that would be, to be able to fight back. Deep within them there was a great ache of anger. They were so very weary of being the victims. Running. Hiding. Begging for mercy where there would be none. Weary of opening tired eyes every morning with the recurring first thought forming in their blurred minds: would this new day be their last, cut short by a sudden visit of obscene atrocity? Perhaps they could find passion and energy again, if they could just have their day of retribution and bring bloody vengeance on the animals who had raped their daughters and destroyed their lives.

At last, the old prophet spoke, his voice trembling as he held the tears at bay. He had chosen each word with care and had repeated this speech twenty times now in his tour of the villages and towns. He would say them again twenty or thirty times more, another year's work, but the only way. 'Thus says the Lord, the God of Israel: "I led you out of Egypt and brought you out of the land of bondage . . . I delivered you from the hand of the Egyptians and from the hand of all who oppressed you, and drove them out before you and gave you their land . . ."' The crowd nodded. Some lowered shame-filled eyes as they remembered again the great story of their fathers' fathers. This story was the reason for the strange longing in their hearts that they had felt, even in the better years; it was a pain that told them all that something, or somebody, very important was missing. The trembling voice continued: 'I said to you, "I am the Lord your God. You shall not pay reverence to the gods of the Amorites, in whose land you dwell. But you have not given heed to my voice."'

The people stood in breathless silence and waited. They knew now that no promise of victory was coming. In fact, perhaps the old man would continue and spell out the curses and judgements that they deserved and, indeed, were living with. Perhaps there was no way back. They waited, some fearful, some shifting their weight uncomfortably, the tension a physical thing, the air thick with anxiety.

The old prophet looked around, searching their faces, and then, without another word, he walked quickly through the crowd and was gone.

❈　❈　❈　❈

Prophets don't always predict the future; sometimes they just tell the truth with piercing, terrifying clarity, a wake-up call from heaven. So it was with God's prophet in the time of the judges. Why should he say anything new? Why would he deliver more words to the ears of a people who refused to hear what God had already said with fire at the mountain, and repeated through the angel at Bokim in Joshua's day (Judg. 2:1)? How many more times would God have to repeat himself?

God repeated himself once more as the prophet, with just a few words, explained the one vital truth that never quite seemed to get through.

Why?

A thousand times as they had run from the fields they had screamed, 'Why? Why is my beautiful daughter dead, her innocent flesh the plaything of perverts? Why was my hard labour of a year destroyed in an hour by these human locusts? Why?'

The prophet spoke to tell the people why things were as they were. Understand, Israel. Learn, Israel. This is the reason for your current condition. *Learn*, Israel! Your unfaithfulness means that your protection has gone; the Good Hand has lifted.

What about us, over three thousand years later? It's so easy to shake our heads in disbelief and tut-tut at the leathery hard hearts of these prodigal people, but why is it that many of us who 'know' the truth about sin and grace still go round in our own wilderness circles in our besetting sins? Why do we allow our feet to get caught up in the coils of the sin that so easily entangles? Flushed and embarrassed from our failures, we vow to do better and renounce for ever the delicious luxury of sin, and then, just mere days later, we run headlong back to those same dirty pools and drink deep once more, our vows like discarded contracts at the muddy poolside . . .

Perhaps the real malady is not so much our capacity for moral failure but rather our tendency to wander away from the person who is called God. 'Prone to wander, prone to leave the Lord we love', as the hymn writer laments it. The more distant we allow ourselves to become from the Father's embrace, the easier it is to feed with the pigs. Sin begins to take root when we lose our intimacy with God. What remains is a lifeless set of rules and regulations but no fire or desire to live them out. Even if we manage by self-effort to avoid straying, we end up in Pharisaism, Christless Christianity, a legalistic morality code and nothing more.

Or perhaps we get taken captive by an overpowering sense of hopelessness when we fail, a sense that we'll never ever be any better, that we are just doomed to this. Ironically, we are then tempted to further rebellion: 'You've already done this, so why not go further? Trash is trash, after all.'

Could it even be that we misuse the very grace that is such a delight and relief to us when we sin? We feel the bliss of the forgiven. We can feel closer to God when still hot from our sin than we do on more pious days. The humbling that we feel in failure can bring a grateful closeness to God that is impossible when we are leaning on our own piety. We ignore Paul's warning and abuse this grace, continuing to sin, that grace may abound (Rom. 6:1).

Perhaps we just refuse to listen, even to God and even though God shouts. We are wilful and stubborn and just want our own wretched way, whatever the consequences. Driven by the madness of self, we record even his rebuke in our spiritual journal, and then raise a clenched fist to the face of God.

Whatever the reasons behind our waywardness, we must stir ourselves and see the deceptive nature of sin.

We must strip away the glossy veneer that coats it because, to state the obvious, sin is only tempting because it looks so very attractive. But beneath the pretty, inviting sheen lies a deadly poison that will lull us into a moral coma, harden the sensitive arteries of our conscience and ultimately paralyse us – for years, if we let it. The very nature of sin is that it seeks to dominate and master us. We must own up to our sin, in a society that seems loath to attribute blame or responsibility, preferring to appeal to the cause of 'mitigating circumstances', upbringing, or indeed anything, to shift the blame off the offender. God refused to allow Israel to pass the moral buck. Canaanite religion may well have been deceptively similar to the true faith, but they were still held responsible for their straying. Israel could have protested their fragile human-ity, claiming that their inability to resist the intoxicating sensualism of Baal worship was a design fault in their make-up, and so was God's fault really. But God held them accountable, and he still demands that, whatever the drawing power of sin in our own day, we make good choices and break out of the depressing cycle: Rebellion. Retribution. Repentance. Rescue. Rebellion. Retribution . . .

Perhaps you find yourself in the 'half-sleep' of poor choices, and have been dozing like that for years. It's time to wake up.

Yahweh brought terrible judgement on the Israel he loved, but he did so for a purpose: he longed to see his peo-ple wake from their slumber, arise and run with him again. But they slept on, which was why the prophet spoke.

❈   ❈   ❈   ❈

The bright summer field had turned to hell. Over and over again the sickles cut and gouged and tore into flesh, a huge harvest of hate. Perhaps the raiders drew special pleasure from using their victims' own harvest tools for the butchery. Terrified children clutched vainly at their fathers' legs, but even they could expect no mercy. Their dying sobs filled the air where laughter had reigned only minutes earlier. Mother Deborah, where are you now? Barak, will you rise again and rescue us?

The woman had stopped running now. She was already dead, even though, physically, she still lived. As if to blot out a bad dream, she had covered her eyes when they took her sons and hacked the life from them, but the awful sound of their retching agony had already driven her over the brink of madness. She stood in the calm of insanity and waited for the raiders to come. Now it was her turn.

Chapter Two

Calling and Commission

The angel of the LORD came and sat down . . . (Judg. 6:11)

The fire was dying, and the large house had become uncomfortably chilly. A couch that doubled as a bed had been placed close beside the fading cow-dung embers. The man they called Joash stretched out his stiff legs and trembled with the cold that comes to a prone body during sleep. Tucking his *simlah* cloak tightly around him in a vain attempt to stave off the late evening cool, he yawned at length. The rest of his extended family must be sound asleep in the bed-chamber. Frustrated with the fading fire, he yelled impatiently for his manservant. Moments later the attendant rushed in with fresh fuel, all flustered and apologetic, but it was too late. Joash was fully awake now, unable to return to his favourite recurring dream. He swung his legs down from the couch and, wiping sleep quickly from his eyes, he looked around the room. Not bad, but the great house had seen better days. As befitted a man of his station, the stone walls were carefully plastered with lime and gypsum, but the fine wood-panelled floors were long gone, replaced by simple clay. In the grate, a lonely flame struggled with the slightly damp dung. Foul clouds of smoke billowed up, most of it escaping through a near-by window, but stinging Joash's eyes as it went.[6] He sat, head in hands, thinking about nothing, just listening. The city seemed quiet, save the distant barking of those wretched dogs that fought every evening over rubbish at the city gates There was something strangely comforting in the familiar drip-drip of water that trickled from the house gutters down to the cistern. Getting up and stretching again, Joash walked over to the wooden-latticed windows and looked out across this city that he thought of as his. His house had one of the most prominent views, as befitted the custodian of the Baal-sanctuary.

Joash was a Hebrew who could trace his roots back to Joseph himself; his name meant 'Yahweh has given'. But now his loyalty was firmly elsewhere, with the Baals. The gods had been benevolent to him, even in the midst of the poverty created by the cursed Midian. What had Yahweh done to help them? Perhaps *he* had deserted them for good. Good riddance. Joash would survive. He had some cattle, and more servants than he needed. He had the respect and ear of the citizens, and deference and honour from those who lived in the outlying villages. Times had been hard, very hard. What remained of the harvest looked meagre, but he hoped that Baal-Berith would bring better days again.

He loved his fair city, the city of Ophrah, meaning 'little fawn'. To the east lay the River Jordan. Eight miles to the south-east, where the Valley of Jezreel narrowed and dipped into Jordan Valley, was the Canaanite-fortified

---

[6] Chimneys were not in use at this time. Smoke, a constant irritation to the eyes (Prov. 10:26) normally escaped through a strategically placed window or door.

city of Bethshan, the 'Great Mound of the Fortress'. In better times they and the other Hebrews had been able to use the dwellers at Bethshan as forced labour. They should have driven them out years ago, but never quite had the muscle or motivation to do so. Anyway, for hundreds of years the people of Bethshan had shown loyal dedication to the goddess Anat, the Baals, and Reshef the god of pestilence – several temples had been built in their honour. Perhaps that was the source of their strength.

It was time. Wrapping his *simlah* around him, he opened the great wooden door, stepped across the threshold and locked the door behind him with a simple, crude key.[7] Hurrying quickly now through the cramped houses of the city, he deftly avoided the rubbish that littered the streets. Wrinkling his nose at the stench, he climbed the steep track that wound its way up to the city stronghold (Judg. 9:51). He smiled as he approached the high place. How fitting it was, he pondered, that the Baal altar and sacred pole should be sited in the place of final refuge.[8] It made a statement: Baal is our garrison, our protection. Joash could hear the bulls snorting in the distance, and now, as he shone his oil lamp over the pen, snorts of hot steam shot from the creatures' thick nostrils into the cold night. The bulls, two of them, were agitated

---

[7] Doors were lockable – see Judges 3:23 – by use of a small wooden bolt arrangement. Six small iron pins would drop into the hollow of the bolt, securing it, and it could only be opened by a flat wooden key with the same exact arrangement of pins. James Hastings, *Hastings Dictionary of the Bible* (Edinburgh: T £& T Clark, 1909)

[8] Usually cities were accessed through a main defensive gate, and had a strong tower, where a last stand could be made in the event of an attack.

at the sight of him. What fine, huge beasts they were, years in the fattening, ready for the glorious feast days to come. One of them would die in just a few days. The heavenly bull above would surely be pleased with such a handsome sacrifice. Joash passed on and continued higher.

Steadily he climbed until he came to the face of what seemed to be sheer rock. The city stronghold was deliberately placed in what appeared to be a remote and unapproachable haven gouged high up in the limestone face, and indeed it was completely inaccessible to the raiders. The men of the city knew the secret footholds, had practised their climb many times, so that they could quickly take to the stronghold in the event that Midian came by. They would scurry up onto the ledge of the high place, and from there, if necessary, into the labyrinth of passages and caves that honeycombed the easily yielding rock face. Placing a practised foot here and there, he was fifty feet up onto the ledge within minutes – a perfect sanctuary, and the ideal vantage place where the Baal altar could be seen at feast time when the whole city gathered. Pausing at the four-foot high Asherah pole which guarded the entrance, Joash checked the oil in the two incense burners either side of the pole. All was well. Soft light danced and flickered upon the rock face, illuminating the teraphim which swayed softly, eerily in the breeze. These clay figures of bodies with real, mummified human heads were popular objects of worship, particularly among those who desired to revere their ancestors. Joash approached the carefully laid altar and checked the pottery incense holder – all was ready. The Baal stories, including the exciting rescue of Baal by Queen Anat, who had snatched him from the clutches of Mot, the god of death, would be carefully acted out as part of the feast. That, together with the glorious orgy which followed, would ensure the fertility of soil, beast and human for the coming year. Joash trembled slightly, life in his old body yet. Excited at the joys to come, he began his slow, careful descent.

❀   ❀   ❀   ❀

It was another, younger man who turned that same key the following morning and set off for what promised to be a tedious day. They were bringing in the small harvest today, and every hand was needed if the grain was to be threshed without the Midianites discovering it. Even though he was the youngest son[9] of the Baal-custodian, the man enjoyed the privileges of rank and seniority – he had at least ten servants at his personal beckoning. But he was always conscious that he walked in his father's shadow: it was father whom the people lauded, not him. Gideon was a nobody, his privileges borrowed.

Today he would join the people in a frantic effort that would ensure the survival of Ophrah for another year. They had chosen an unusual threshing site – the old winepress out by the *terebinth*, the sacred tree, on his father's grazing land. It was too dangerous to use the community threshing floor at the edge of the city. There the oxen would make quick work of the task, dragging great threshing sledges lined with stone teeth to separate the grain from the hulls. Sometimes they would have the cattle shod with special shoes and allow them to stamp out the grain. It was so much easier on high ground

---

[9] Gideon's later protest that he was the 'least' (*ts'ayr*) in his family suggests the likelihood that he was the most junior in age – see Judges 6:15

where they could immediately winnow the grain. The western evening breeze would then blow the chaff away, while the heavier grains of wheat or barley fell at the winnowers' feet. But today, the threshing floor would lie empty, and the old winepress instead would be a hive of frantic activity. The crop was too small for the threshing floor anyway, and the risk of discovery was too great. Gideon hurried on to the old oak.

A small group of men had already begun the work, hurling the sheaves down into the press, little more than a deep basin cut into stone, and then taking it in turns to step down to thresh. No sledges or oxen here – they used a threshing stick literally to beat the ears of corn and separate the grain. Another man hurried to gather the beaten ears. There was a steady hum of conversation in and around the stone pit. Anticipation was building about the Baal festival, just days away now.

Gideon greeted the men, and then stripped quickly for work. He had no time for idle chit-chat, and was eager to get the work done and get the precious grain out of sight. At last he took his turn to step down into the winepress. It was less than ideal for this work, but at least it provided a flat, hard surface. As he stepped down into the stone vat and the shadows of the old tree fell across his back, did he remember the stories of his youth – tales of the God who would sometimes appear to people under trees? As he began his long, back-breaking day of work, did he recall that echo from long ago when Father Abram had built an altar to Yahweh by the great trees of Mamre (Gen. 13:18)? Then, he had heard, God himself had come and stood beneath those same trees, and wizened Abram had rushed off to prepare an offering meal. When he returned, Yahweh had announced that Abram's worn-out wife Sarai would have a son (Gen. 18:10). The story went that Sarai had laughed and laughed at the very idea of pleasure at her age . . .

Or did the sight of that tree cause him to recall the much more recent saga of Mother Deborah, just twenty-five years or so earlier, who had sat beneath the tree known as 'Deborah's Palm', in the hill country of Ephraim, and there spoke wise words to those who would hear (Judg. 4:5)?

Did Gideon look up at the high place of Baal and Asherah, distant now, yet dominant still on the skyline, and feel sudden resentment and confusion clash within him as he took in that sight? He had always been so appalled at the gross orgies that followed the feasts. They seemed to violate something deep within him, but he didn't know what it was. He had no faith in the Baals, and yet he couldn't find Yahweh. Did God still appear in the soft shadows beneath the trees? He smiled at the foolishness of the thought. Yahweh was gone. But somehow he couldn't let Yahweh go . . .

The stories he had heard in childhood thrilled and disturbed him at the same time. If they were really true – and no one denied they were – then what were they doing worshipping the Baals? As he began to work, an ache of confusion settled on his mind, nagging at him, refusing to go away. Then he felt a sharp sense of irritation at his fellow workers, as they loudly boasted of exploits and conquests to come at the feast. Pushing the thought about Yahweh forcefully from his mind, he took the threshing stick more firmly in hand. Perhaps there was the anger of humiliation. Every year, the marauding tribes subjected the Hebrews to the same annual indignity, not bothering to possess the land completely. It was easier to allow the Hebrews to do the back-breaking work of harvest, and then swoop when the crop was gathered and snatch it out of their hands. Or was it the humiliation of having to take the threshing stick in his hand? This method of threshing was traditionally only used by the poor when they 'knocked out' their meagre quantities of grain (see Ruth 2:17). Perhaps grief had turned to rage: two of Gideon's brothers had been brutally murdered, apparently by Midianite princes, at Mount Tabor (Judg. 8:18,19). They did not die a warrior's death in battle, but as victims of a raid. The men around the winepress noticed that he was beating the grain with unnecessary force now, anger burning in his eyes . . .

Quickly, no time to lose, throw another sheaf onto the stone, man. Strike it now, strike it now, strike it hard. Punish the grain, beat it into life. Foolish this, threshing in a winepress. Winepress. The place of joy. The place to shout with delight when the grapes are brought in. Where was the joy now? Why this lingering sadness, even when Midian stays away? What is it that the old prophets of Yahweh had said about the wine-press?[10] Yes, that was it, that Yahweh the vengeful judge would trample out the grapes of wrath, judgement for unfaithful Israel. More corn now, hurry . . How my arms ache already, how this awkward threshing stick cuts into my hands and makes the skin sore . . . Beat it, thrash it, thresh it, food for our children . . . Like a father beating a wayward child, like Yahweh beating and threshing his people, judgement, judgement, judgement . . . Quickly man, another sheaf and make it fast . . . Sweat in my eyes, but keep beating; anger and frustration and fear a driving pulse within me; muscles taut and my whole body now bathed in sweat. Judgement. Judgement. Winepress. Thresh the wheat. Thresh the wheat. Abram. Deborah. Brothers, dead now. Angels. Baal. Father . . .

---

[10] Lamentations 1:15; Joel 3:13. Both were written five hundred years after Gideon's time, but I am assuming that the concepts of winepress wrath and threshing judgment were already in Hebrew thinking. If nothing else, I can claim poetic licence!

He paused, and squinted up into the sunlight that tumbled lazily through the branches of the old oak. No, it was not his imagination. There was a man sitting there, in the soft shade of the tree. A stranger, or at least a face he didn't recognise. How dare he! Didn't he know that everyone was required to work from dawn till dusk today, no excuses? He looked around at his fellow workers. Apparently they hadn't noticed the stranger, or if they had, they ventured no comment. Was he hallucinating, the relentless glare and heat playing merry tricks in his head? He looked again.

It was a man.

And he was smiling.

❋   ❋   ❋   ❋

Freeze the frame right there. Let's pause for a while and look a little closer now, and wonder. God himself has dropped by to see Gideon. Look at how he comes. Consider this life-changing meeting. A sweaty, nervous man peers anxiously into the gloom beneath the great tree, his forehead wrinkled in confusion. What does he see? A shimmering, blinding white hot light bursting from the base of the sacred oak? Liquid holiness like a great lava flow filling the winepress and burning Gideon up in its white-hot cauldron heat? The majestic yet gentle spread of snow-white angel wings, huge, yet impossibly delicate? Perhaps a halo of dancing rainbow colours circling a face of indescribable beauty?

Actually, perhaps Gideon saw a stranger sitting comfortably, leaning his weight back against the thick tree trunk; a man relaxing. No thunderbolts in his hands; no lightning flashing from his eyes.

What does he hear? The exquisite song of ten thousand cherubic voices, the finest choir in the history of the universe, their hosannas entwined in a glorious weaving of heavenly harmonies? Or perhaps a thunderous, booming bass voice that shakes the ground and causes a terrified Gideon to press his palms vainly against tortured ears and beg for mercy?

No massed choir. No earthquake voice. In fact, no song and dance at all. God doesn't produce Cecil B. DeMille-style special effects in order to arrest our attention. And that's the glory of it.

He comes to our boring days. He refuses to live in the sacred box that we would make for him. He may, of course, be found by those who seek him in special buildings where majestic architecture, painstakingly and lovingly crafted centuries ago, still prophesies his presence in stone. He may be discovered dancing towards us on the soaring melodies of haunting music. A fleeting glance of him may be seen in the shifting shadows as the altar candles flicker their soft light. We may smell his scent in the heavy fragrance of incense that perfumes the air with mystery. All of these things can be part of a helpful drama that allows us to look for the Mighty One in our technologically overloaded, sterilised world. But we mustn't lock him up in those places, lest we shut him out of our ordinary days spent in more mundane places. This Lord of ours has a habit of showing up with surprising news in unusual locations, to the people we would least expect.

Be careful, says the Scripture, about the way you treat strangers – they may be angels (Heb. 13:2). So be hospitable. The glory may be heavily disguised. That person who comes by and appears to need your help may well be hiding his wings so that he can help you.

❋　❋　❋　❋

Now look at the one God visits; look at Gideon. He is not the earnest-faced intercessor, facial muscles locked in serious, pious concentration as he performs acts of intense religious devotion. He's a bored, frustrated labourer stamping around fearfully in the winepress, doing ordinary stuff, when an ordinary-looking God – at least at first glance – shows up with some extraordinary information.

The God we serve bypasses the royal court of Herod and the mighty palace courts of Caesar, choosing instead to draw a weary bunch of shepherds on night shift into his confidence. Admittedly, on that occasion, it *was* more of a firework display as the Lord ripped back the canopy of heaven to reveal a partying angelic host. There again, that was not an evening for quiet restraint. The birth of Jesus was the *ultimate* reason for throwing a huge party. And then, as God rolls out redemption's story, he grabs the attention of an engaged carpenter and his teenage, virgin bride-to-be. He is the God of the ordinary person. Consider the common feeling of *being ordinary* that snaps around our minds. The sense that we are just run-of-the-mill, nothing special, just like the rest of the herd. And so we are. But God comes to the run-of-the-mill, nothing special herd.

I find that fact incredibly comforting, because there are times when I feel an acute sense of my plain *ordinariness*. Don't tell me that the Bible continually makes it clear that even the greatest heroes of faith are just flesh and blood like the rest of us. I still feel that I should be something else or somebody more special. I look into those glossy Christian magazines, with their colour photographs of impossibly handsome or beautiful men and women of God. Their fixed grins seem to imply that they are camped continuously right next to the very throne of God, and as I peruse their gleaming, confident smiles, icons of certainty, I feel so human. Fragile. Flawed. What a relief it is to discover that even those who look so together actually have feet of clay.

I discovered that again, to my joy, when attending a major leaders' conference a few years ago. Even the name of the conference was vaguely intimidating: 'Bionic Apostles and Prophets Together for the Universe', or something like it. I made my way to the dining room and sat opposite a woman who looked incredibly mighty. She had 'Woman of God' written all over her. She was quietly eating the meal lovingly prepared for her by the Christian conference centre *chef de cuisine . . .*

Crisis struck. I immediately felt ordinary. This woman probably knew Leviticus off by heart and had cast out demons before breakfast. I ventured to introduce myself, 'Er, hello, my name is Jeff. Jeff Lucas.'

I expected her to look up from her meal, heaven ablaze in her eyes, and say with the authority of the sage, 'Yes, I know. I saw you in a vision in 1953.'

She did not say anything of the sort. She just greeted me with a bright hello and warmly introduced herself.

'Have you had a good week?' I ventured, more for something to say, really.

'No, it's been terrible. Awful, in fact.'

I struggled to look compassionate and sympathetic, but inwardly my heart soared. Good! Ms Mighty in God had had a rough week. That meant that she was normal, and that all circumstances did not immediately jump to her intercessory command.

'Er, what went wrong then?' I inquired hopefully. The dear lady then described how she had taken her family to the car wash. During her attempt at mechanical ablutions, family style, a major personal crisis developed. It appears that Ms Mighty in God had put the token in, noted that gratifying moment when the big brushes obediently start spinning and the water jets begin to advance relentlessly towards you, and then decided to check that her car window was shut tight. She flicked the window handle, which immediately came off in her hand. Then, to her total horror, the window fell down all the way, disappearing inside the door, leaving a huge gaping hole which would surely facilitate the admission of thousands of gallons of warm, sudsy water. They would all be drowned! The woman looked around her car in a vain search for something, anything, to put into the gaping door to prevent her car from becoming a cross between Noah's Ark and the *Titanic*.

There was only one thing that she could find that would provide a suitable watertight seal, which was . . . her own bottom.

I really tried not to laugh, but the very thought of it made me want to lie on the floor and kick my legs in the air. Part of my joy was the release that came in knowing that, yes, this was a woman who really loved God and had his authority upon her life. And this was a person who, just like me, knew how to do idiotic things, knew how to be absurd, probably knew how to be scared, knew how to be defeated. She was ordinary. I am ordinary.

Move over, Gideon. Is there room in your winepress for two more?

❊   ❊   ❊   ❊

Gideon looked again at the seated, smiling figure. Just who was that man? We might ask the same question. Was it an angel? Yes. Was it the Lord? Yes – twice the narrative declares, 'The *Lord* said' (Judg. 6:14,16). What was going on?

Though Gideon didn't know it, he was actually having an audience with a person described as *Melek*

Yahweh, 'the angel of the Lord'. Commentators have had a field day of speculation trying to set up an identity parade for this messenger of God. Some say that he is a theophany – an appearance of the eternal pre-existent Christ – while others describe him simply as the chief and primary angelic representative of Yahweh on earth.

What is clear is that it is difficult to make a distinction between the Lord and the angel of the Lord, such authority and power does he carry. The fact that he receives worship and offerings shouldn't trouble us or lead us into angel worship. The angels always come as the messengers of Yahweh, and in eastern thinking, homage paid and hospitality given to the messenger was homage paid to the one who sent him. Later Jesus used that idea when teaching about relationships. Give someone a cup of cold water, and we give Jesus a drink. Take time to go and see the downtrodden one in jail, and it's Christ who receives the prison visit (Mt. 25:35 ff.). What a different world we'd live in if we treated every person we met as one sent from God and worthy of respect and kindness. It's not just a nice idea; it's the way we are supposed to live.

The angel of the Lord shows up frequently in Scripture: comforting traumatised Hagar in the desert (Gen. 16:7-13); burying himself in the heart of a burning bush that became a life beacon for Moses (Ex. 3:2); appearing with a sword before Balaam's pathway and seriously upsetting his donkey (Num. 22:22). Some years before Gideon's time he had addressed the nation of Israel at Bokim (Judg. 2:1), the place of weeping, and had warned the trembling crowd that the hand of God would lift if they continued in their rebellion. It appears that one of his major tasks is to bring comfort and confirmation to the faithful people of God. A beautiful heavenly scene is depicted in Zechariah, as Joshua meets *Melek Yahweh* and gets a change of clothing, removing garments that were stained by sin and receiving new, fresh grace clothes (Zech. 3:1). But the angel of the Lord is also the bringer of judgement upon the unfaithful and the blasphemer – Herod learned that lesson the hard way. He was instantly eaten up by maggots when he got beyond himself – a terrifying touch from *Melek Yahweh* (Acts 12:23). A few years after the Gideon story, the same angel would appear at another threshing floor and exact a wholesale slaughter of David's people as an act of judgement (2 Sam. 24:16). But when he appeared to Gideon, there was no sword of vengeance in his hand. On the contrary, he brought a simple message of good news that was to change Gideon's life for ever.

❀   ❀   ❀   ❀

Perhaps Gideon put his head down and carried on working, ignoring the apparently idle stranger. There is certainly no record of Gideon initiating any conversation. It seems that, initially, he had no idea as to the true identity of his visitor. He would later address him as 'sir', a polite term of respect, but probably nothing more. Finally, the moment came. Gideon was stooped down over the corn ears, beating away, when at last the man spoke.

When angels speak to you, everything changes. Hagar's tears are dried, she stops running and starts to live again. It would not be the last time that an angel dried her tears (Gen. 21:17). Elsewhere, the angel of God speaks, and the quivering knife raised in agonised Abraham's hand is stayed mid-air, and Isaac breathes again (Gen. 22:15). Throughout the pages of Scripture there are so many occasions when angels appear and speak just a few words, and everything changes in a moment.

Gideon had been hiding in a winepress, trying to make the grain 'vanish' from the sight of Midian. But if Midian was fooled, God knew where Gideon was. He came by, sat down and spoke. In a few seconds, a man's heart and life were turned around.

❀ ❀ ❀ ❀

Gideon shook his head, wondering, perhaps for the second time, whether he was dreaming a waking dream, hallucinating, a victim of the relentless sun. Then he realised. The mystery man was speaking, but the others didn't appear to hear his voice. Gideon looked up. The man was looking at – and speaking to – *him*.

Chapter Three

The Crisis of Good News

'The Lord is with you, mighty warrior,' the angel said.
And Gideon said, 'But sir . . .' (Judg. 6:12,13)

What do you do when an angel arrives? Fall on your
face in an expression of unrestrained adoration? Burst
into tears of joy and amazement? Allow a stunned
silence to settle over you, your mouth wide open as you
gaze on the heavenly visitor?

Gideon seemed to greet the messenger with a measure of frustration. He shook his head in irritated disbelief. Just who exactly was this madman who was
stretched out lazily under the tree? Was he a lunatic, or
a drunk perhaps? What wild, foolish words he spoke.
The LORD is with you, mighty warrior . . .

Yahweh, with us? Impossible! Had the strange
traveller not heard of the awful atrocities that Midian had inflicted with such sickening regularity? It
was the numbing fear of further attack that had
driven Gideon and his colleagues to the winepress in the
first place. So who was this sarcastic stranger who
apparently had stopped by to mock them in their afflic-
tion?

Had this fool not heard the words of the old prophet who had made his rounds so recently? Some had trembled at his words, most had dismissed him as a ranter, but no one suggested that there had been a hint of hope in his message.

The LORD is with you, mighty warrior . . .

Mighty warrior. *Gibbor hayil.* The term used to describe a band of noblemen famed for their prowess in battle. Hardly the expected greeting for the trembling Gideon; no sword in his hand, but a threshing stick hurriedly wielded. He manned no battle station, but hid away like a nervous fugitive. Even Jewish tradition, which sometimes tends to gloss over the humanity and failings of biblical heroes, refuses to paint Gideon as a strong man. The rabbis didn't teach that Gideon was brave. It was their belief that Gideon was chosen by God for his particular role in saving the people because he had been a good son to his father. A legend circulated that when Gideon's father was old, and fearful the Midianites would attack and kill such an aged prey to get his grain, Gideon had told his father to go home. 'If the Midianites come after me, I am fast enough to run away.' It is interesting that he did not say that he would stay and give his life for his father's grain. Mighty warrior? Not according to the rabbis.

The LORD is with you, mighty warrior . . .

This was too absurd. Whoever this weird stranger was, he was looking for a serious argument.

❊   ❊   ❊   ❊

In a world of painful video footage and depressing news flashes, our God, by contrast, is wonderful news indeed. I have always felt slightly uneasy when passing by those stern-faced and undeniably sincere men who yell

Scriptures at pedestrians and hold up their placards that scream 'Repent or burn!' in black gothic script. At one level their message is true, and yet Jesus came with a message that is such *good* news that the word 'gospel' ('good tidings') is the summary word for the message of Christ. 'Comfort, comfort my people . . . Speak tenderly to Jerusalem,' says the gentle God to his servant Isaiah (the Hebrew word means 'to whisper sweet nothings . . .'). God loves us with a passion that defies logical explanation.

Brennan Manning refers to a scene from *Gideon*, a play written by a Brooklyn Jew named Paddy Chayefsky

> Gideon is out in the desert in his tent a thousand miles from nowhere, feeling deserted and rejected by God. One night, God breaks into the tent and Gideon is seduced, ravished, overcome, burnt by the wild fire of God's love. He is up all night, pacing back and forth in his tent. Finally dawn comes, and Gideon in his Brooklyn Jewish accent cries out, 'God, Oh God, all night long I've thought of nuttin' but you, nuttin' but you. I'm caught up in the raptures of love. God, I want to take you into my tent, wrap you up, and keep you all to myself. God, hey God, tell me that you love me.'
>
> God answers, 'I love you, Gideon.'
>
> 'Yeh, tell me again, God.'
>
> 'I love you, Gideon.'
>
> Gideon scratches his head. 'I don't understand. Why? Why do you love me?'
>
> And God scratches his head and answers, 'I really don't know. Sometimes, my Gideon, passion is unreasonable.'[11]

---

[11] Brennan Manning, *Lion and Lamb – the Relentless Tenderness of Jesus* (Chosen Books, 1986), pp. 96–97.

And how lean is the soul that has never been romanced by the passionate Lord. Donald McCullough laments the tragic Marilyn Monroe.

> Marilyn Monroe has become a kind of icon – a symbol, in a way – of the sensuality and emptiness of our time. Arthur Miller, in his autobiography *Timebends*, tells of his marriage to her. During the filming of *The Misfits* he watched Marilyn descend into the depths of depression and despair. He feared for her life, as he watched their growing estrangement, her paranoia, and her growing dependence on barbiturates. One evening, after a doctor had been persuaded to give her yet another shot, Miller stood watching her while she slept. 'I found myself straining to imagine miracles,' he reflected. 'What if she were to wake and I were able to say, "God loves you, darling" and she were able to believe it! How I wish I still had my religion and she still had hers.'
>
> But Miller had no religion, no God to love and protect his beloved in her growing lostness.[12]

Certainly the angel brought Gideon a message from God that was unexpectedly wonderful, and Gideon put up a protest. Why could he not just submit and obey as Mary did, and why do we so often follow in his footsteps? I believe that there was more than fear and hopelessness in Gideon's heart. The dialogue with the angel leads me to believe that a sinister cancer had crept in, a deadly tumour called cynicism.

❈   ❈   ❈   ❈

---

[12] Donald McCullough, *The Trivialisation of God* (NavPress, 1995), p. 20.

The preacher was really working up a sweat now. Fire blazing in his eyes, he hurried urgently along the long line of waiting, praying people, their hands extended before them, their eyes tightly shut, focused on another world. Within minutes the worshippers became skittles, their bodies scattered haphazardly. Watching from three rows back, my mind raced. What was the source of this persistent nagging question mark that gnawed away at my brain, flitting around my head like a humming mosquito? My nervousness had begun earlier, during the preaching. Apparently the speaker had just returned from 'phenomenal', 'extraordinary' meetings in India, where, and I quote, 'hundreds of thousands of blind eyes had been opened, and hundreds of thousands of deaf ears had been unstopped'. I had quickly stifled the irreverent thought that such an avalanche of miracles would surely have put the relatively unknown speaker on the front cover of *Time* Magazine . . .

Now, as he ministered, the nervousness returned. *Why does he have to hit them so hard when he prays for them?*

That was it. I didn't mind his impassioned, theatrical shouts, 'In the name of Jeee-sus!', as he raced along, or the comical positioning of the catchers as they tried to figure out which way each body was going to fall, their arms out, waiting for the next crumpling. I honed in on the source of the niggle. *He was hitting them, ramming the palm of his hand into their foreheads, and then pushing their heads back at an angle.* My mind skipped and danced between anger and guilt: angry, and mildly depressed, at the apparent circus trickery that so desperately needs someone to fall down that a good shove is in order; guilty, for even thinking such a thing about this man of God. Was this just his style? Closing my eyes, and covering my ears, I tried to pray, and hoped that it would be over soon . . .

I describe this real moment for you because it demonstrates a common dilemma. When God moves, some people throw open their arms and seem willing to take on board anything that comes along, while others clench their fists and fight what they don't understand.

We rightly fear cynicism, the cancer that so readily strikes the hopeful. The cynical heart is freezer cold, unable to be warmed by the God who really does come and work among his people. Cynicism takes the tender-hearted worshipper and turns him into an arms-folded spectator, a scowling analyst with a clipboard and stop-watch under his arm and a bless-me-if-you-dare expression on his face.

But a simplistic, thoughtless naïveté is waiting for us at the other extreme. Unquestioning, we take on board every prophetic word, regardless of content or spirit. A new 'revelation' is shared, and despite feeling an urgent sense of disquiet, we bury our concerns, not wanting to be perceived as critical or 'out of the flow'. This silent pressure to conform can be very intense in an atmosphere of spiritual enthusiasm – like a church pursuing revival. It's like being carried along by a huge football crowd: your shoulders are pinned tight, your feet lifted off the ground, a hapless passenger of the consensus. We feel guilty for even considering the possibility that something might be wrong. Surely, if everyone is going with it, can they all be mistaken?

It's the most extreme example, but the fact is that everybody *was* wrong the day they drank orange squash laced with cyanide at the infamous Jonestown. But a similar power of peer group pressure can bid us to silence our questions and concerns. We don't want to line up with the critical people who rush to the publishers any time that God shows up, and we certainly don't like the Judas the traitor/Thomas the doubter feeling that rises up when we ask awkward questions. So we stay silent, and worry quietly.

Is there a pathway between these two extremes, a so-called 'healthy' scepticism? I believe that there is, and that there is a biblical demand to walk on that middle ground. As Paul wrote to his friends at Thessalonica, we are to 'test everything, and hold onto the good'. This command comes immediately on the heels of Paul's warning that we should not 'put out the Spirit's fire, or treat prophecy with contempt'. So this testing is not seen as a negative, doubting response to the work of God, but rather as a positive duty for those who would feel the heat of Holy Spirit flames and hear his voice through the prophets.

We create an environment where this testing can take place when we encourage people to ask questions – even if those questions are difficult at times – in order to find clarity and authenticity. Whenever God moves, question marks are scattered all over the place. The Day of Pentecost brought an outbreak of power and a rash of questions and misunderstandings. 'What does this mean?' the crowd asked. We'd do well to take the time to join them; sometimes I wonder if those of us who are charismatics know how to *feel*, but not how to *think*. But Jesus told his wonderful little stories in order to provoke his listeners to ask questions, so that in the mental wrestling and the cut and thrust of debate, we discover.

Questions save us from gnostic meaninglessness. There have been quite a few times when I have wanted to interrupt a prophet who seemed to be making nebulous pronouncements: 'You say that we are on the edge of the third breakthrough in the heavenlies as we embrace the hallmark of the new thing God is doing for the hungry and thirsty, but what do you mean?'

We will also need to guard our attitude as we question. Paul Reid says that churches are hindered by   people who have 'an opinion about everything and a heart for nothing'. What's the motive – and the starting point – for our questions? Do we inquire out of a desire to prove the badness of something, or rather its goodness?

Cynicism also flourishes when our expectations are unrealistic, which is a common problem among idealists like us. We all have unspoken expectations about the way things should be, and rightly so. But we can forget that those we walk with are flawed human beings, just like us. If you've been in a church for more than six months, and nothing about it or nobody in it has ever irritated you, then you're probably clinically dead. We do need to adjust our hopes into line with a realistic understanding of the frailty of human nature.

There's only one way to stay balanced on the tightrope between unbelief and unhelpful simplicity: it takes grace. And my conclusion on that heavy-handed evangelist? Well, he might be anointed – perhaps, but I'd like to see some Indian medical reports. And he should stop shoving people around.

❈   ❈   ❈   ❈

Cynicism doesn't need a second invitation. It is an epidemic disease that is being found more and more among those who used to be called the hopeful. What shall we do with it? Find the more perfect church? Wait until all of our struggles and difficulties are resolved? Is there a way out of the winepress? Do we stay in chains until a blinding flash of supernatural light fills our gloomy cell? Actually, even the supernatural will not melt the cynical heart. The professional religious leaders stood outside the tomb of a man who had been buried long enough to stink. They heard a man called Jesus tell the corpse to live again. They watched with their own eyes as the man struggled, impossibly, out into the light, his putrid graveclothes pungent testimony to the death that had been. Then those same leaders, blinded and deafened by their cynicism, went off and held a committee meeting. Item number one on the agenda was, 'Getting rid of this Jesus'. Take it from me: the sight of a miracle or two, or even a ringside seat at the raising of the dead, won't shift cynicism. In fact, a move of God will harden the hearts of the cynical. When God comes, the hopeful become more hopeful and the Pharisees become more pharisaic! A move of the Spirit doesn't solve the problem of cynicism, and ironically, it may make it worse.

There is a way out, but we might not like it. The only escape from cynicism is through repentance. Cynicism is sin. Repentance is the only way to deal with it.

Make a choice, Gideon, and all of us who are like him. Step out of that place. Elijah had to vacate a cave, Gideon a winepress. Come on out. It's boring, dark and lonely, and not much, if anything, is going to be achieved in there.

Step out now. Step back into believing that you can and will make a significant difference with your life once again. 'You will save Israel,' said the angel, impossibly. And if you feel inclined to linger in cynicism for a while longer, remember who it is that speaks to you. Perhaps, as the conversation continued, Gideon's eyes were being opened to the true identity of his visitor, and so the angel declared:

'Am I not sending you?' And that's the bottom line. The dwelling place of cynicism is not a luxurious option for those who would follow God. He tells us, in no uncertain terms, to get out of there, and get out of there now.

But for Gideon, there was another chain that bound him to the winepress.

Whereas cynicism is an inability to trust and believe in God or God's people, insecurity is an inability to believe in the value of oneself.

Gideon suffered from both.

❋   ❋   ❋   ❋

The Lord is with *you*, Gideon.
Gideon, *you* will save Israel.
I am sending *you*.
Go in the strength *you* have.
Yes, Gideon . . . you.

❋   ❋   ❋   ❋

Gideon was selected for significance – and struggled with the very notion that he could be of real use to God. We share his insecurity, reading in Scripture about those mighty women and men of biblical history whom God used in the past, but disconnecting that sense of usefulness from our little lives. We thrill at the books that chronicle God's goodness in the lives of others, but we are less convinced about the possibility of such things happening where we live. And we sing majestic, moving songs about God's love for the world in general and everybody else in the world in particular, yet the truth is that so many *Christians* live lives apparently unaffected by that love.

It isn't that we don't believe that God is love; it's just that we are less sure that he loves *us*. That was Gideon's problem. The personal emphasis is emphatic in the

Hebrew: 'The Lord is with *you* . . . *you* will deliver . . . in the strength *you* have . . .' The crisis point came when Gideon was invited to believe that the mercy and grace of God was upon *his* life. That was the real shock. Perhaps that's why God's bottom line message to those he calls is always, 'I am with you.' That's what he said to mumbling, send-someone-else Moses, to trembling Joshua and to Jeremiah. That was the parting speech of love that Jesus gave to his disciples before rejoining his Father in heaven. I am with you. Perhaps that's why God says it in the letter to the Hebrews with such repetitive force: 'I will never, never, never, never, never [five times in the Greek text] fail you nor forsake you' (Heb. 13:5).

And typically, Gideon protests that he is not up to the job.

He is graphic in his self-dismissal. 'Our clan is the least in Manasseh.' The word for 'least' contains the idea of dangling, dishevelled hair. Perhaps Gideon's put-down on himself could be better translated 'We're the bad-hair-day tribe'!

There are only around one hundred verses in the Bible that relate to Gideon's life, and a great number of them are specific to dealing with the monstrous insecurity that Gideon seemed to suffer from. Dealing with the Midianites was easy for God. As we'll see later, you just thin down an army, arm them with candles, glass jars and trumpets, and get them to break the aforementioned jars while yelling at the tops of their voices. The enemy will obediently turn on each other, exacting wholesale self-slaughter while you just mutter an occasional 'Praise the Lord'. The Midianites were nothing compared to the huge sense of insecurity and self-loathing that lived in Gideon. Why such a massive inferiority complex? Well, to understand that, you have to go back in time a few hundred years . . . unless it was just because he was the youngest brother!

❋   ❋   ❋   ❋

A thousand years earlier, a poignant family scene was taking place. Jacob, or Israel ('the prince with God'), as he had become known, was not far from death (Gen. 48). It was customary for the children of the dying to gather for a final blessing, but Joseph, Jacob's favourite son, was paying a visit to his ailing father in advance of that larger gathering. Joseph made the trip because he sought a blessing for his two sons, Ephraim and Manasseh. The blessing of the father was a serious matter, and none knew that more than old Jacob. It was he who had managed to steal his brother Esau's birthright blessing years earlier. Disguising himself with the dress and the smell of the hunter, he had received the blessing of *his* father, Isaac, and once the blessing was given, it was irrevocable (Gen. 27). Now the time had come for the old rogue to bless *his* grandsons.

Joseph brought Manasseh and Ephraim into the darkened chamber, and carefully sought to choreograph the occasion. Pushing his sons forward to the bedside, he put Manasseh at Jacob's right hand. As eldest son, Manasseh was the son who was in line for the primary blessing. The right hand was the place of blessing, the place of honour (1 Kgs. 2:19; Ps. 110:1; Lk. 22:69; Rom. 8:34). The left hand was used to hold a shield in battle. Step to Grandfather's right, Manasseh, and now, Ephraim, you stand at his left. That's right. Perfect.

What was it that caused old Jacob to do what he did? Was it some vague memory of his own dirty deed, so many years earlier? To Joseph's surprise, he crossed his hands across the boys' heads, and placed his right hand upon *Ephraim's* head (Gen. 48:14). Manasseh, in that moment, was passed over. Second place. And perhaps the tribe named after him never forgot that moment. The language that Gideon would use later suggests that Ephraim was always held in higher esteem than Manasseh (Judg. 8:2).

Now, an ordinary man from a passed-over tribe was being asked to save Israel. The hand of God was stretched out, wanting to place a blessing upon Gideon's head. No wonder he was shocked and amazed. God was *for* him.

❈   ❈   ❈   ❈

The approval and affirmation of God came as a shock to Gideon, but these were far more than nice words from a friendly God. These words were designed to provide a solid backbone for the nervous man – life, muscle and energy were imparted in the message. 'Go in the strength you have, and save Israel,' said the angel. These words are very often misunderstood. The English translation seems to give the impression that God was commanding Gideon to begin his mission in his own strength, and that the strength and power of God would be added later. Nothing could be further from the truth, and if we quickly skip over the text, we could miss a vital lesson here. The word of command – 'Go in the strength you have' – is connected, welded with the word of promise: 'the Lord is with you'. In other words, Gideon was being asked to *walk in the strength that he had as a result of the revelation that God was with him*. Feeling weak, timid, terrified, Gideon? Here's muscle for you: God is with you!

Strength and confidence are ours when we know that God has determined to walk beside us with a smile.

Perhaps that's why Jesus chose the words 'I will be with you' as his final parting speech to his fearful disciples just before Ascension Day. The knowledge of his presence, of his blessing, is the source of our strength to face an uncertain future. God had to shout his approval at fearful Gideon. He's been shouting something similar at me lately, too.

❊ ❊ ❊ ❊

I believe that God is for me – at least, academically and theologically, I'm convinced. Just like Gideon, however, I have my winepress moments when God seems far away, and then, however many scriptures I may have memorised that tell me I am loved and approved of, I find myself vacillating, and groping around in the fog of fear. God is very kind to me, and so in recent years I have found myself on the receiving end of his shout of approval. As often happens, God's voice to me has come through obedient people who have bumped into me and sensed a need to prophesy into my life.

The shout began in California. An attractive lady with a broad smile came to me at the end of a great service and, with a certainty that I sometimes find unnerving, announced, 'I have a word from the Lord for you.' Outwardly I returned her smile, and inwardly I groaned. I'm sorry to say that I am frequently accosted by well-meaning charismatics who proceed to tell me that they have the proverbial word from the Lord for my life. Some of them do. Some of them don't, but are sincere. And some of them are just strange. Too many times I've been forced to concentrate desperately and fix my facial muscles to prevent myself from laughing out loud when presented with yet another bizarre 'prophecy'.

'I've got a picture of a yellow jellyfish, Jeff. He's tap-dancing on a tin of Ambrosia Creamed Rice, and he's whistling "I'm a Yankee doodle dandy" . . . '

Then comes the question that I quite literally fear:

'Does this mean anything to you?'

I've had more than my fair share of this kind of madness, and so I'm sad to say that I tend towards scepticism – and sometimes the cynicism that I described earlier – when I encounter yet another budding prophet who wants to try out their seer skills on me.

So when the nice Californian lady announced an imminent 'word from the Lord', I braced myself for another trip into the surreal world of charismatic behaviour.

The lady was unaware of my inner turmoil, and so continued. 'During your preaching tonight, Jeff, I had a picture of the Lord Jesus.'

Panic raced into my heart, and two opposing thoughts wrestled somewhere inside my head. Thought 1: This is not authentic. She needs medication. Thought 2: This is authentic. God is going to get me. The Jesus that she is seeing has probably got fire coming out of his mouth and a sword of judgement in his hand.

I said, nodding calmly with eyes half-closed in sublime spiritual contemplation, trying not to express any hint of what was going through my mind, 'Really. What was the Lord saying and doing then?'

The lady chuckled. 'He was laughing, Jeff. He was looking at you and then he threw his head back, and he just laughed and laughed. He looked at you with such love. He enjoys you and what you do so very much, you know. He thinks that you are really very funny. God loves you!'

Suddenly, my Ambrosia scepticism fled, and I wanted to cry. How marvellous that Jesus would go out of his way to assure me of his love and pleasure. Amazing. Particularly when you think that he has heard some of my material over and over again. Omnipresence has its drawbacks . . .

I was encouraged – thrilled even – for a while. And then, pressurised by ministry and travel, I quickly forgot the moment.

A few days later, in the West of Scotland this time, I was packing my books away at the end of a service when a lady approached me. She was the wife of a Church of Scotland minister. She seemed nervous.

'I've got a word from the Lord for you,' she announced, and I immediately had a picture of creamed rice. 'Really? Thank you. Please tell me about it,' I replied.

'I need to say this privately,' she stammered. 'Would you mind stepping outside?'

Now I was bracing myself for a yellow jellyfish in a tartan kilt tap-dancing on a tin of Baxter's Royal Game soup. Obediently I walked to the door, and stepped out into the downpour that seemed to echo the feelings of my heart. Here we go again . . .

The lady began, a hesitant tremor in her voice. 'During the worship time tonight, I saw Jesus. He was standing in front of you, and then he began to dance and shout. There was such a smile on his face, Jeff. God wants you to know just how much he loves you.'

Inside me, it stopped raining. Suddenly the sun came up, somewhere inside my chest. She continued, nervous still, unaware as she was of the abrupt emotional weather change that her words were bringing.

'The Lord knows that many harsh things have been said to you lately by people in his church. He wants to wash those things out of your hair, and soothe your tired brow.'

I was thrilled, and was then immediately panicked by her next words.

'God wants me to act this word out, to help you to receive the message. This is what God says to you. I'm very embarrassed about this, but I do need to obey God.'

And there and then she stretched out her hands and began to stroke my forehead!

War broke out inside me. Something deep inside me knew that this woman was for real. Her obvious embarrassment and deep humility helped me know that there was nothing remotely sensual or compromising about this moment, but my ability to receive the word of the Lord was very definitely hindered by an overwhelming fear that, any moment, one of the delegates from the conference would walk out and discover me having a happy moment with the Church of Scotland minister's wife. But that night, God let me know in a very vivid way – so vivid that I will never forget it for the rest of my days – that he was *for* me, that he *loved* me. Having just written this down, I suppose that I still fear the possibility that some readers will misunderstand, will discard all of this as madness. But know this: as I recall the event again, I find myself strengthened by the knowledge that God loves me. I am walking in the strength that comes from that revelation.

There was a third shout. I was in Eureka, California. Bethel Church, until recently led by Ken and Debbie Frank, is one of my favourite churches in the world. They have faith-fully risked everything in their desire to make Christ known in a meaningful, intelligible manner; their worship of Jesus is wild and enthusiastic. I was about to preach on the right hand of God's favour, speaking, as it happens, on the Jacob/Ephraim/Manasseh story mentioned earlier in this chapter. No one in the building knew my text or my intention. Seconds before mounting the platform,

Linda Abercrombie tapped my elbow and whispered in my ear. Linda has a remarkable prophetic gift, and manages to balance her anointing with a refreshing earthiness that is both winsome and engaging. I have learned to listen to her when she says that she has heard from heaven.

'Jeff, would you please give me your right hand?'

She had no idea of my subject, could not possibly know the significance of her unusual request. But I gave nothing away, and simply asked why she wanted to hold hands.

'God has just told me to anoint your right hand with oil. I know it seems bizarre, but perhaps it makes sense to you . . .'

Makes sense? I felt as if heaven was roaring out a thunderous shout of joy and approval, as minutes later I stood up to preach about the right hand of God's favour, with my own right hand dripping with oil. It will come as no surprise to report that the Holy Spirit swept through the place that night in one of the most memorable meetings of my life.

❋ ❋ ❋ ❋

Slowly the truth dawned inside Gideon's racing mind.

There was something very special about this stranger. How wrong he had been to dismiss him as a mad fool. There was authority in his voice, confidence beaming in his smile. There was something awesomely fearsome about him, yet winsome and wooing too. He felt that he wanted to be around this stranger some more. Perhaps he thought back to those stories of angels appearing to his forefathers long ago. When was it that the staggering truth appeared as a coherent thought, gathering strength and clarity with every passing second? Was it when the stranger promised that he would be with Gideon in the challenge against Midian? How could a mere man just walk into Gideon's life and promise to be with him, at his side continuously? The argument with the traveller stopped, and was replaced with a fiercer bout inside Gideon's mind.

Perhaps the stranger was just a madman.

Perhaps he was a prophet.

An angel, perhaps.

And then the thought crashed into Gideon's frail mind like an explosion.

Perhaps he was talking to God.

❋   ❋   ❋   ❋

It might have been that he was cynical – certainly he was insecure – but Gideon was called to step out of passive defeat and stand bravely against the forces of evil. We can easily relate to his weaknesses, but then we consider what he was called to do, and the gap widens between us and him, and the similarities stop. He was called to be a high profile hero, the primary leader in the nation. Most of us won't ever occupy such key positions of power and influence. I am nervous of the impression that is often given at large Christian events – particularly at events involving young people – that we are all called to be the next Billy Graham, or even that 'the ministry' (whatever that is) or so-called 'full-time Christian work' is the 'highest calling', the most productive way to live your life.

The reality is that the King is establishing his kingdom through millions of faceless people who will never undergo theological training, place 'Reverend' in front of their name, step into the spotlight or develop as smiling evangelical celebrities. They are the ordinary folk who quietly decide each day that they want to be salt and light in their dark communities. Through their daily choices, satanic altars are quietly and systematically demolished. Because of the influence gently exerted by the ordinary faithful, the kingdom of God breaks out in life-transforming power. The future is not in the hands of the articulate people who stand on platforms, and I say this as one who spends most of my life on one platform or another. But as a Christian leader, I am not on the 'front line' in God's holy war. I am a member of God's ordinance core, privileged to help, serve and resource the real heroes who today will be faithful to God as hospital workers and home-makers, mechanics and managers, school teachers and secretaries, or – an even greater challenge – as those unemployed, wrongly deployed or just holding down what can only be described as boring, mundane jobs. They are the unnamed thousands who tiptoe through their Christian lives balanced on the high wire between cultural relevance and radical, salty, slap-the-culture-in-the-face discipleship.

For Gideon, the winepress represented survival and existence, grain for yet another sad day. But he was born for something far more satisfying. And there are many like him, who will not spend their one life on a treadmill of going to work, to get the money, to buy the food, that gives you the strength, to go to work, to get the money, to buy the food . . . They are the true 'Gideons' who have turned their backs on mere existence and have embraced life, and abundant life at that. Perhaps you are one of them. Or perhaps you used to be, but have somehow stepped down from life and settled back into survival again. As you believe in the God who is willing to believe in you, you discover a life that is truly living. If your current address is a winepress, it's time to vacate it and move on.

Chapter Four

Puppets or Partners?

A Jew is a person who is in travail with God's dreams and designs. (Rabbi Henshall)

Consider your next move, angelic one.

You've managed to grab the attention of the nervous little man from Ophrah. His eyes are finally beginning to open. He thinks he knows who you really are. Faith, like a tiny embryo, is forming in his heart, an impossibly fragile, growing seed of life. Your shocking announcement is sinking in. He seems willing to co-operate. Consider your next step, Lord.

Perhaps a map and a detailed set of instructions would be appropriate. A line by line itinerary charting every step of his mission. Lay out your intricate strategy. Bark the orders. Spread out the plan. Be the commander-in-chief. Speak.

Wait!

Pray silence now. The little man has a suggestion to make.

'I need a sign that it really is you talking to me . . . I'll get an offering. Please don't leave. Will you wait?'

Perhaps the angel smiled. Certainly he quickly responded: 'I *will* wait until you return.'

As Gideon hauled himself quickly out of the wine-press and rushed down the track towards his home, a million questions dancing around his mind, one thing was certain. The man, the angel – the Lord? – *would* wait. It would take a little while to prepare the offering, but however long it took, the traveller would be as good as his word. For no earthly reason that he could think of, Gideon knew that he had just met a stranger whom he could trust his life to. And back in the shadow of the tree, God sat and waited for an hour or two. For Gideon. Ponder the wondrous sight. I said God waited. For Gideon.

❊   ❊   ❊   ❊

Let's take a 'fast forward' look at the next few episodes in Gideon's life. There will be time to examine them more later. Speeded up, the facts are these:

Gideon is staggered that grace could light up a wine-press that had been shadowed by moments of gloom ear-lier. He wants to make a response, and. so asks to bring an offering to his now-welcome visitor. The Lord agrees to the proposal, and waits long enough for Gideon to round up a kid goat and hastily bake some bread dough. Some while later Gideon returns to the winepress, laden down with a meat basket, a broth pot and some fresh bread under his arm. God is waiting under the oak, but Gideon obviously needs something more to bolster his confi-dence. The Lord commands his newly enlisted servant to present the offering by placing the meat and the bread on a rock. The broth was to be poured out.

Suddenly the old oak becomes a place of genuine ter-ror as God extends his staff and torches the bread and meat in a blinding flash of light, as fire springs up in a second from the rock. The smoke clears and Gideon's courage vaporises along with the charred goat meat. And then Gideon realises that the Lord has disappeared completely. Fearing that the sudden disappearance may signal judgement, and realising fully that he has had an audience with the living God, he is seized with terror. Death seems likely and imminent. Then a voice speaks soothing words of peace to the traumatised Gideon, who is mightily relieved, and builds an altar called 'peace' to celebrate his relief. The Lord then tells Gideon to take an axe to his father's altar and make his stand for the true God. Gideon is willing, but scared, not of God now, but of his neighbours who will not take kindly to the desecration of their occultic shrine. Gideon makes another suggestion. He *will* destroy the Baal shrine, but under the cover of darkness, out of the sight of prying eyes. The Lord agrees. We'll examine this more closely later, but for now, consider with me the idea that trembling Gideon is no mere puppet in the clutches of his Maker. Rather he is being invited to step up to a grace position that is far more dignified. He is being invited to become a partner with God.

❊ ❊ ❊ ❊

Tragically, there are some Christians who are appalled at the idea that God would want to partner his people. Their theology paints a black and white portrait of a God who is somewhat transcendent, aloof even. For them, he is the static, fixed, unmovable being at the centre of the universe who, to quote the theological terms, is *transcendent* and *immutable*. No skip or spring in the step of this God. No dancing shoes on his feet. Rather, he is the ramrod stiff general, eternal medals dazzling on his swelling chest. Or perhaps he is the Victorian father, the papa who lines his trembling children up at the end of the day for a pre-bedtime inspection. Or maybe he is the absolute dictator, fêted and adored by nervous minions.

There is no possibility of warm interaction, never mind relational negotiation, with the general-papa-dictator God. He barks commands. We jump to attention. *'Yes, sir!'*

But there is a major problem with these mutated concepts of our God. The Westminster Confession states that 'man's chief end is to know God and enjoy him for ever'. Enjoy a dictator? Relax with the stiff papa? Love a dictator, with all your heart, soul, mind and strength?

To *love* such a God is difficult, if not impossible.

I know. I tried.

I wasn't a Christian for very long before I heard the well-worn adage 'God has a perfect plan for your life'. The idea of a blueprint came to mind, an intricately detailed set of drawings laying out the proposed existence of one Jeffrey Richard Lucas on planet Earth. But I did not find the blueprint idea comforting, or inspiring, even though I was thrilled with the idea of purpose and destiny. What worried me was the very real possibility that I would make a mistake or take a wrong turning, and miss the plan. I would then be consigned to live on the spiritual scrap heap graphically described by the preacher as second best. I became frantic, obsessed even, to find out the will of God for my life. My motives were genuine – I really did want to follow the elusive plan – but I nearly lost my mind in trying to find it. I purchased every book on 'Knowing the will of God' that the local Christian bookshop had on its shelves, having prayed frantically that the book I would read would be the one that it was actually God's will for me to read, of course. Often, what I read compounded my sense of terror and fear. It all seemed like a 30,000-piece jigsaw puzzle, with a good two or three hundred pieces missing, held back in the hand of a God who seemed to delight in leaving me in the dark of confusion.

The Bible, apparently, was one of the major pieces of the puzzle. 'If you want to know what God's will is, then pray and just open your Bible. It's there in his word. Simple.' It *did* sound simple. The reality was a complicated nightmare. I took those words of counsel literally. Kay and I had just met – she is now my wife – and I urgently, *desperately* wanted to know if she was 'part of the plan'. Open the Bible, they said. God will speak about whatever you're praying about, they said. I threw open my Bible to a random page, and stuck my finger on the lines of text. Unfortunately my finger hit Proverbs, which sternly warned me about consorting with prostitutes. I was horrified!

Then I discovered the bewildering notion of the absolute sovereignty of God. I was told by someone that inevitability was built into the very fabric of the universe. As one writer put it, 'No one or nothing can resist or frustrate his sovereign will. It will inevitably come to pass.' This apparently extended to the most minute detail. Roll a dice, and the two sixes that make twelve were actually pre-ordained from the beginning of time. Play a game of Cluedo, and know that somehow God set it up that Miss Scarlet committed the dastardly deed, in the study, with the revolver. God apparently has an opinion about everything. To quote another theologian: 'There are no areas that fall outside the purview of his concern and decision.'[13]

My choice of clothing, the place where I shop, the items I purchase, the people I speak to in the shop . . .

---

[13] Millard Erickson, *Christian Theology* (Baker Book House, 1998)

all part of something called the predestined will of
God.

Chance? No such thing. In a fixed view of God, nothing is by chance. To quote the old chestnut: the hyper-
Calvinist falls down the stairs, picks himself up and
sighs, 'Thank God I've got that over and done with.' As
another writer says (incredibly): 'Would you like to
know God's sovereign will for the past? Well, if something happened, it was part of the plan.'

That makes God ultimately responsible for the
slaughter of the innocents at Dunblane; his 'loving' hand
shifted the monstrous, moving hillside of Aberfan that
engulfed a school during assembly time and silenced the
lilting song of a village's children in an instant. The murder of Holly and Jessica, 9/11 . . . all 'part of the plan'?

If this were true, what kind of God was I following?
Not only that, but why bother to seek his will if it will
ultimately come to pass anyway? In fact, why bother to
pursue prayer, sacrifice, holiness, evangelism, or anything that demands effort and commitment, if ultimately
it's all going to work out according to the sovereign master plan? And I know that I am treating a huge subject
– the sovereignty of God – in a very simplistic manner,
and risk upsetting my Calvinist friends in the process,
but these were the conclusions that I came to as a new
Christian.

It got worse. I read somewhere that the easy way to
know the will of God was to look for a sense of peace in
my heart. This peace, the books assured me, would be
like an umpire in a cricket match, the final referee and
arbiter of all decisions. This teaching was mainly based
on Paul's exhortation to his friends at Colosse: 'Let the
peace of Christ rule in your hearts' . . . (Col. 3:15). The
problem with this concept was two-fold. First of all, Paul
is writing to the Colossians about relationships in the

local church. His statement has got nothing to do with personal guidance whatsoever. Secondly, this put me in a circle of confusion, where the subjective state of my emotions became the ultimate referee of the game of life.

I wanted this elusive sense of peace, but my lack of this 'magic' peace created more and more agitation in my heart. Thus I was unable to be at peace!

Then someone tried to help with the remark, 'God will open and close the doors for you.' That sounded good, if not a little fatalistic. But which doors were opening because God was turning the handle? What if Satan was opening a door of deception, or barring a door of genuine opportunity? What if more than one door opened? Help!

I tried to sit myself down and calmly think the whole thing through. And then another bright person – who may have had previous work experience as a friend of Job – advised me that these things were not logical, so I might as well forget the idea of reason and logic. The mind was fallen, he said. 'Lean not on your own understanding,' he quoted from the book of Proverbs, completely ignoring the fact that Proverbs is a book that encourages us to become people of wisdom. The acquiring of wisdom is celebrated fifty-one times in that book. But for me, the development of wisdom was replaced by a desperate search for revelation. I kissed my brain goodbye, and continued in quiet, fearful panic.

But the worst was yet to come. The Exocet that almost sent me over the edge was the advice from a well-meaning friend that 'the will of God is probably the way you would prefer not to go. Whatever *the flesh* would prefer *not* to do is probably his plan.' I couldn't work out exactly what part of me constituted *the flesh*. I concluded that I was pretty much 100 per cent flesh, so whatever I liked, God didn't. Whatever I didn't like, God was into. This left me with a severe problem about Kay. Strangely, I was going out with her because I liked her. She was fun, easy to be with, attractive, and she really loved God. I knew I really liked her, and dared to wonder if I might be in love with her. And at that thought, fear rushed in like a whirlwind. *Whatever I liked, God didn't.* This relationship must therefore be wrong. I would have to give her up, and find someone less agreeable, less attractive, and thus please the God who just longed, apparently, to wipe the smile off my face. I went to the front at the end of a hundred services and wept. On one occasion, I actually repented of feeling happy, feeling that a lightness of heart was incompatible with godliness. I developed a twisted view of a God who spent all his time dreaming up nasty little plans. Looking back on it now, and with the benefit of having children of my own, I can see how warped my thinking was. Imagine Richard, our sports-loving son, asking for a basketball hoop for Christmas. And there I am, late on Christmas Eve, wrapping a set of heated curlers for him. I'll give him what he neither needs nor wants just to see if he still loves me . . .

I have a sense that there will be many readers who will have nodded their heads in recognition during the last dozen or so paragraphs. You too nearly blew a mental fuse over this issue of the will of God. Are there any simple principles that can help us out of this labyrinth of confusion? The trembling hero in the winepress can help us. Gideon was called to fulfil God's purpose – a man called to a mission – and so he is a prototype for all of us. Most Christians I know desperately want to participate in God's broad game plan for the earth. Perhaps a peek into the winepress will help us.

❋   ❋   ❋   ❋

The will of God is found in God

'The LORD is with you, mighty warrior.'

We've already seen that this was more than a pleasant religious greeting. This was the key that unlocked Gideon's future. God does not offer Gideon a scroll of instructions, or a map of directions. He offers Gideon himself.

One of these days I'd like to write a book called *Stop looking for the will of God*. With such a title it would never become a best-seller, but I believe that it could be sound advice. No doubt the title would irritate myriads of well-meaning Christians whose whole lives have become one long spiritual safari, ever hunting down the elusive will of God. While it might not be popular, it might well be biblical, for I can't find too many exhortations in the New Testament – or in the whole Bible – to search out and seek the *will* of God. Rather we are encouraged at almost every turn of the page earnestly to hunger and thirst and seek for God himself.

When guidance, rather than the God who guides, becomes our preoccupation, we are in danger of engaging in evangelical 'mystic Megism'. We yearn for direction. Long for instruction. Ponder the future. Consider our destiny. And in so doing, we can end up in a subtle idolatry, worshipping the will of God rather than God himself.

Gideon had a future because he had God. Moses knew that principle, and baulked at the idea of going into the Promised Land if the God of promise wasn't going to go with them. For Moses, blessing without the Blesser was unthinkable.

Stop looking for this impersonal thing called God's *will*, and spend your energy in loving and looking for

God himself. As you offer yourself to him, Scripture promises that you'll then know the will of God (Rom. 12:1,2). Gideon took time and effort to offer an extravagant *minchah* meal to the Lord. In a time when grain was obviously in short supply, Gideon presented over twenty-two pounds of bread! Throwing thrift to the wind, he rolled out the red carpet of hospitality to his heavenly visitor. Follow his example. Find times of quiet to love God, and in those moments of intimacy God can mould you to fulfil his purposes, whether you are aware of it or not. Those of us who, like myself, love our worship to be of the loud, colourful, flag-waving, pull-all-the-stops-out variety need to rediscover the value of silence and retreat. As we take time to love God, we fulfil his primary and prioritised will for our lives. As Thomas Kelly[14] writes: 'God never guides us into an intolerable scramble of panting feverishness.' Without that intimacy, we end up with a 'McDonalds' spirituality', a popcorn piety that stumbles from one great celebration meeting to another, a loud superficiality. We rely on good music, fine preaching, the roar of the crowd, and never know the peace that only solitude brings, the order which is the fruit of godly discipline, the calm that is spawned by silence. God waited in the winepress, because there Gideon rediscovered what was really important. The tangled priorities that had fought in his heart were unknotted in those winepress minutes and hours. We need the same. As Gordon Dahl says, 'We tend to worship our work, work at our play and play at our worship. Our relationships disintegrate faster than we can keep them in repair, and our lifestyles resemble a cast of characters in search of a plot.'

---

[14] North American Quaker

However, lest we sit around having indulgent times with God while a lost world stays lost, we also need to remember that we are called to be servants as well as lovers of God. When we came to Christ, we began a relationship that carries a two-headed calling – friendship and function. God met Gideon, and flowing out of that encounter God gave Gideon a task. That's the way God works with all of us. Jesus invites his disciples to follow him (friendship) and then promises that he will make them fishers of men (function). God reveals himself to Joshua (friendship) and then calls Joshua to get up and cross the River Jordan (function). And so it is with Gideon: 'The LORD is with you, mighty warrior' (friendship), 'Go in the strength you have' (function). I labour the point, because it is important that we see it. Every thing goes wrong in our Christian lives when these two elements of our faith are not in harmony together. The *friendship-centred* Christian who loves to sing worship songs and read their Bible, but has no desire to dirty their hands in evangelism or get involved in meeting the needs of their community, is an irrelevant ostrich whose prayers will soon become hollow rhetoric, because they don't echo the mission heart of God. The *function-centred* Christian may hurtle themselves around working for God, but will collapse and burn out because their activity is not being sustained by an inner life that revolves around God. And so it was that Gideon was called first to God, and then to the purposes of the God who is strategist. He knows where he's going, and wants us to travel with him.

The ancients had a dangerous saying: 'Love God and do what you like'. At first glance, the statement sounds like a licence to sin. But think about the wisdom of these words. If we *truly* love the Lord, then our hearts will be turned to the things that please him; his hopes will become welded into ours; his character and beauty will be formed in us.

Are you on a hunt for guidance and direction? End the treasure trail. Put away the desire to find the 'x' that marks the spot. Look rather for the living, breathing, loving God who longs to walk *with* us, rather than just give us marching orders.

❋   ❋   ❋   ❋

The will of God is in the words he has spoken

The angel delivers the good news: God is with you. Gideon furiously volleys a question back: 'But if the LORD is with us, why has all this happened to us?' At first glance, the question seems reasonable, until you stop and remember that God had already given the answer. In the Law, now much neglected, God laid out his covenant treaty. Obey me, and I'll bless you. Forsake me, and I will lift my hand of protection from you. The law of cause and effect, laid out clearly and plainly. But this was not just an ancient decree long forgotten, buried in a scroll somewhere. The Spirit of God had inspired that unknown prophet to reiterate the principle. In other words, Gideon was asking a question that God had already repeatedly answered. And so God did something perfectly reasonable. He totally ignored the question.

If we think that Gideon must have been completely stupid, consider that Christians repeatedly do the same. Scripture has been given to us as a revelation of God's broad, moral will. You won't find out where to go on holiday by dipping your finger into Leviticus, or the name of your future marriage partner by reading Hosea (though some have tried other pretty bizarre techniques), but you will discover certain inviolable commands that God has revealed in Scripture, which he is never going to change. Scripture makes certain issues plain. It is never the will of God to cheat, blaspheme, gossip, intentionally wound others or engage in sexual immorality, to quote a few obvious examples out of thousands. God's will is in his word.

This is why it is so very important that we are people whose thinking is permeated by the principles of Scripture. When I first became a Christian, I was instructed to read the Bible and pray every day, but I wasn't sure why this regimen of study was so important. It appeared that the devotional habit was an evangelical form of saying the rosary. Apparently God would be pleased if I performed this rite and ritual every day, and apparently, the earlier in the day that I did it, the happier he would be. But there was great practical wisdom in it. Study of the Scriptures is vital in that it provides a nourishment for our hearts that cannot be found anywhere else. It is imperative because we are given the opportunity to pause in the swirling mists of relativism and pluralism and a host of other 'isms', and bring our lives and our minds to the straight edge of divine truth. And the God-breathed Scriptures also provide us with an opportunity to engage with God's heart, to sense the scent of his breath and to ponder his eternal wisdom. When Scripture plays little part in our lives, we end up asking embarrassing questions that have already been answered.

The will of God is discovered in the dignity of partnership

The winepress episode reveals a God who works out his will in a variety of ways. Sometimes he just gives a command, like the broad instruction to Gideon to stir himself and become a saviour for Israel. Scripture is full of similar examples of God speaking to his people and simply issuing a non-negotiable command. Paul dreams a prophetic dream and receives orders from the Holy Spirit to go to Macedonia. Moses obeys a voice from a burning bush. Followers of God are under orders, and God, being God, may demand and command at any time. But we are wrong to think that the command is the only means that God uses to work out his will. At other times, God allows his servants to offer suggestions. The sacrificial meal – and the confirmatory signs – were Gideon's ideas. This remarkable sight of the God of the universe taking suggestions from his puny people is not limited to the winepress episode. Moses, who was also told that the Lord was with him, was privileged to make suggestions in prayer. When Moses is high up the mountainside having an audience with God, the people down in the base camp below get restless, hold a jewellery party and then decide to worship the golden calf idol they have just made. Moses comes hurtling down the mountain with words of divine judgement ringing in his ears – God has decided to put the people to death. Moses, ever the patient pastor, cries to God, and suggests that the death penalty is not such a good idea after all. Moses uses a rather unusual argument in his prayers. He suggests that the notion of God killing people would not look good! Incredibly, we read that the Lord relented, or repented. God agreed to the proposal offered by the courageous Moses! The sight of God heeding the suggestions of his servants is just too much for some commentators. One writer suggests that when God told Moses he was going to kill the people, he didn't really mean it. He just said it in order to make Moses pray according to the predestined will of God, and then the Lord would be able to respond by doing what he always intended to do in the first place. At best, it's a complicated idea, and at worst, it seems that God told Moses a lie. But as Frethren puts it, 'God was inviting Moses to contribute something to the divine deliberation. God was open to change.' Isn't it simpler – and incredibly exciting – to consider the reality that God listens to his people, and is willing to make changes to his plans accordingly, as well as telling them what to do? Certainly that was Moses' and Gideon's experience.

If that idea worries you, because you fear that God would be sharing the government of the universe with fallible, fallen people, think again. God is committed to doing just that one day, when those people are restored to their perfect state; so does it seem unreasonable for him to start apprenticing us in that role now?

The winepress episode also includes negotiation. God wants Gideon to demolish the wretched Baal altar. Gideon is willing, but would rather do the job under the cover of darkness. Will that be all right, Lord? God responds positively.

And so the story continues to unfold. It is not a monologue – God speaking, commanding and Gideon rushing to obey. Rather we see the remarkable sight of God and Gideon interacting, dialoguing, negotiating. Undeniably, God is the senior partner, the authority figure in the relationship. But he is not, as one writer puts it, a metaphysical iceberg, a static, unmovable, monolithic 'I am'. The God at the winepress is more like a ballerina, sweeping across the stage of human history, gifted, exquisitely graceful, sure-footed. The God who is revealed in Scripture, and specifically in the story of Gideon, is not the unreachable, untouchable, just-do-what-I-say-and-don't-ask-questions God.

Rather, this God spins and pirouettes up to a club-footed, fearful wallflower like Gideon, extends a hand and pops the question: 'Would you care to dance?' The glory of the winepress shines as we realise that God chose to entwine himself and his purposes with a fearful, stumbling Gideon. Think of it – God risking his reputation on the faithfulness of Gideon! It's a glory that is exhilarating, and leads us to a dignified doctrine of the church, as we partner with God. And as we thrill at the thought, we tremble at the responsibility. If we are more than puppets, partners even, then so much of what God does both now and in the future is depending on our willing response. Suddenly the will of God is no longer a pre-set blueprint, but an interactive adventure.

Donald Baillie adds the analogy of play to dance, describing human life as 'a tale of God calling his human children to form a great circle for the playing of his game'. Frustration is ours when we exclude ourselves from the game.

> In that circle we ought all to be standing, linked together with lovingly joined hands, facing toward the Light in the centre, which is God ('the Love that moves the sun and other stars'); seeing our fellow creatures all round the circle in the light of that central Love, which shines on them and beautifies their faces; and joining with them in the dance of God's great game, the rhythm of love universal. But instead of that, we have, each one, turned our backs upon God and the circle of our fellows, and faced the other way, so that we can see neither the Light at the centre nor the faces on the circumference. And indeed in that position it is difficult to join hands even with our fellows! Therefore instead of playing God's game we play, each one, our own selfish little game . . . Each one of us wishes to be the centre, and there is blind confusion, and

not even any true knowledge of God or of our neighbours. That is what is wrong . . .[15]

Dancing with the Lord. Hurling ourselves headlong into
his great, hilarious, epic game of games. This is our destiny.

❊   ❊   ❊   ❊

Permit me another pause in the Gideon story, if you will,
because I want to share an episode from my own experience that gave me a glimpse of the notion that God
wants partnership with us, a relationship that includes
command, suggestion and negotiation. It was just over
twenty-five years ago, and the second day of our honey-
moon. Kay and I were staying just outside the West
Sussex city of Chichester, where my grandmother had a
house. We were happy and poor in about equal quantities – an exotic vacation was out of the question on my
minister's salary, and so we were grateful for the loan of
my grandmother's house. On the Sunday morning we
drove into Chichester, and stopped to cross the main
A27 dual carriageway. As we waited for the traffic lights
to change, I turned to Kay and said, 'Kay, if I could ask
the Lord for anything, I would like to request that he
gives us a ministry preaching and teaching across this
country and the world, and that we would be able to
base that ministry in this city of Chichester.' Apart from
relatives, we knew no one in the city at that time, and as
for international preaching, we were leading a tiny congregation on a housing estate in the Midlands. I had just
started preaching on Sundays to the twenty-five or so

---

[15] Donald Baillie, *God was in Christ* (Charles Scribners and
Sons, 1949)

faithful who gathered, but I had no public speaking experience and had never preached to any other church, except the odd assignment in Bible college to kindly congregations who allowed us to use them to develop our skills.

Twenty-five years later, having spent five years living in Southern Oregon, we now have a home in the city of Chichester, and both Kay and I are members of Revelation Church, which didn't exist when I stopped and dreamed at the traffic lights. So what happened while the light was red?

For years I believed that God had quietly dropped that thought into my mind; that he had initiated the idea, planting the seed of desire in me, and then delighting in fulfilling the desire that he had begun in the first place. It never occurred to me until recently that it might have been that the idea did not begin with God but with me. Is it possible that the Lord heard me verbalise that dream, and then determined to bring it into reality?

Today I am more excited about living in the will of God than I have ever been. I don't have too much faith in my own ability always to get it right – the reverse is true. But I do believe that God has a deep desire to walk in friendship and partnership with me; sometimes I sense a command, and other times there is room for suggestion and negotiation as I take another spin around the floor with the Great Dancer. Frankly, I feel like a Mephibosheth really. He was the chap who suffered terrible disabilities, but David cared for him, placing him in the seat of honour at parties. I'm not impressed, metaphorically speaking, with my own dancing skills. But my Partner is a genius.

❋   ❋   ❋   ❋

The will of God: memorable moments and red-letter days

Gideon set the meal down. The man *had* waited for him; the costly meal and hurried preparations had not been in vain. In the hurry of the cooking, perhaps Gideon had forgotten that he had asked for a sign. He just felt the need to honour this man, this God . . .

The angel, the Lord, had not forgotten the request. Time may pass between our asking and receiving an answer, but with God, the requests are never forgotten or ignored.

'Pour the broth out on the ground. Put the bread and the meat on that rock over there.'

Throw the soup away? What was wrong? Was the stranger displeased with the meal? Mind racing, Gideon did as he was told, the flat, smooth rock an altar now.

The angel reached out to bless, to confirm, to assure but not to eat. White-hot heat leapt from the cold rock as the tip of the angel's staff touched it. Goat meat and bread literally went up in smoke in a millisecond. Perhaps jumping back in alarm, Gideon cried out. And as the smoke cleared, and the smell of charred flesh and burned bread filled the air, Gideon realised that the stranger had disappeared with the meal.

❋   ❋   ❋   ❋

So why the pyrotechnic display? After all that hard work and self-sacrifice from Gideon, why torch the meal? Why didn't the visitor from afar go ahead and *eat* the food spread before him, as Abraham's visitors had done long before (Gen. 18:8)?

This meal was never for eating. Something of a far more lasting nature was taking place here. God was giving

Gideon a moment that he would never, ever be able to forget, a red-letter day, a moment that would serve as an enduring memory that would repeatedly strengthen Gideon in difficult days ahead.

The meal itself was unforgettable, because of its value. It was an outrageously generous feast prepared by Gideon in a day of famine. Perhaps this moment gives us some insight into Gideon's generosity. This was the man who had named his first-born son 'Jether', meaning 'abundance'. Was he a man who loved to celebrate, who delighted in hospitality, who would have felt the rigours of famine more harshly than most? Now, in this offering, he was giving abundantly, a moment to savour. Every time Gideon counted the goats in his care, every time Gideon considered his meagre stock of grain, he would remember . . .

The fire that sprang so suddenly from the rock would brand itself upon Gideon's memory as well. Any stranger could eat. Only a special Stranger could cremate the meal in a moment.

A mark would remain where the food had been. As one eminent commentator writes

> There must have been a black spot on the winepress rock, where the fire had burned, which would have remained many days in the dry harvest season as a continuing reminder. The spot may well have constituted the rock as a place to revisit in days to come for reassurance that God had really called him. That black, burned spot could have come to mark for him one of the most precious places in all the world, in later days of wonderment, discouragement and opposition.[16]

---

[16] Professor Leon Wood, *Distressing Days of the Judges* (Abingdon), p. 207

The instant flash of fire would transform just another ordinary day into a red-letter, a pivotal, life-changing moment when everything is different because of something that God has done. We all have red-letter days of one kind or another, and they don't have to include angelic visitations or fire bursting from rocks. Those of us who know and walk with Christ have known days of decision, days of breakthrough, days of understanding or revelation – days that make us what we are now. And sometimes, if our faith is really weak, God decides to scorch a rock.

I had been a Christian for about twenty-two days when I had one of my red-letter days. My conversion had been sudden and dramatic, at the age of seventeen. I was immediately gripped by this incredible message of the love of God, even though I did not know the difference between the Old Testament, the New Testament and the maps at the back of my Bible, within the first few days of being a follower of Jesus I was sensing a tug in my heart, an inner call to preach and become a Christian leader. I told a close friend in our church about this vague feeling of destiny that just wouldn't go away. He wisely counselled me to wait and pray and respond to God in his good time. A few days later we went off to a youth weekend. A man called John Barr was due to address us during the weekend. John was the leader of another church in our denomination, but came to our weekend as a stranger to us. On the first night he delivered quite a shock. In his introductory comments, he said something like this: 'As I was driving here this afternoon, the Lord spoke to me about three young people whom he has called into ministry. He told me your names, first and last names. God has already been speaking to you. This is confirmation. I'll speak further about this over the course of the weekend.'

I can still remember sitting there with two thoughts screaming through my mind. First, that this was very impressive and second, who could this refer to? I looked around the room – that person there, they know their Bible really well, or maybe it's her over there, she's considered to be very wise and quite a mature Christian . . . And despite the inner wooing that had been going on inside me, it never occurred to me that the strange man might be talking about *me*.

Twenty-four hours later, we were gathered again in the library of the beautiful old house. We were in a terrific time of worship, when suddenly I felt the strangest sensation, like power coming upon me, forcefully, pushing me down. Then I felt the strangest desire to speak in tongues, something I'd never done before, although I'd heard others do it in our church. I wanted not only to speak, but to speak out loud. It was as if I had a message.

John Barr stood up. 'Someone here is being filled with the Spirit, and God wants you to give a message in tongues. Don't be afraid. Go for it.'

I was spooked. This guy apparently knew everything. But I was too scared to respond. A few minutes later, the strange feeling had gone. The meeting concluded, but I felt very guilty. I had let God down. I should have responded. I went up to John, waited my turn patiently, and then, without introducing myself, launched into an apology for my stubbornness. Aware that I was a new Christian, John encouraged me, and I thanked him and turned to walk away. It was then that he touched my shoulder and said, in a matter-of-fact voice: 'Your name . . . your name is Jeff Lucas, isn't it?'

Right at that moment I wasn't really sure what my name was, but I soon recovered sufficiently to affirm that, yes, my name was indeed Jeff Lucas. John smiled, and continued. 'God has been calling you into ministry, hasn't he Jeff?' Well, er, yes, he had, but look here, surely . . .

'Get on with it then, son,' said the East Ender, and walked away. John has talked about our encounter in many places since. He had never met me or heard my name before, but God had spoken to him. And I heard, and rushed off and threw myself under the bedclothes. I was thrilled and terrified and amazed at the fact that God knew me, and had spoken to me. Within a couple of years Kay (aged sixteen!) and I were planting our first church.

If anyone is tempted to envy this somewhat dramatic experience, or think that I must be really anointed to have such a clear calling, let me tell you why I believe God shouted so loud. It's because he knew my deep fears and insecurities, and so he hollered from heaven in order to cut out most of the wrestling match.

Perhaps Gideon would return to the old winepress again and again, and run his hands over the fading scorch mark. The mark of the fire was the reason for him to step out of mediocrity and stand up for God. The mark might well have sustained him on days when his prayers seemed futile. When doubt threatened to drown faith again, perhaps he made the pilgrimage to the rock.

※　※　※　※

The will of God in our lives: living in the whole revelation of God

When the fire had flared without warning, perhaps Gideon leapt back against the old oak, temporarily blinded by the terrible light, the impossible heat a blast to his face. Did he sit there stunned, rubbing his eyes back into focus, the charcoal odour of super-heated flesh and bread hanging in the air? He looked at the table-like surface of the rock, more an altar now.

The bread . . . gone.

The basket of goat meat . . . gone.

And then he realised. The Lord was gone. There was absolutely no room for doubt any longer. The awful, awesome truth exploded in his mind, which recoiled at the thought. He had been dining with God. It was too much to take in. Gideon did what came naturally. He started screaming.

The cry started deep down inside him and emerged as a frantic sob of anguish, his voice echoing around the old winepress, an eerie, haunting litany. Over and over again he screamed out the words that seemed impossible. 'Sovereign Lord . . . I've seen the angel of God *face to face!*'

Perhaps he threw himself down into the old winepress, pushing his face flat into its unyielding floor in a vain attempt to get away from the certain judgement that he feared was now imminent. Would there be another white-hot finger of flame from the rock that would consume him now in a second? Perhaps every thought of normal life, like harvest, family or the Midianites, fled in that moment of genuine terror – Gideon just felt that the curtain of eternity had been hauled back, and the God of power had stood just a few feet away. Surely only one thing remained now: death.

Why the terror? Hadn't the Lord been kind to Gideon, providing him with such a memorable sign that day? Some commentators suggest that Gideon's theology would have insisted that anyone who sees God will die as a result (Ex. 33:20), although Abraham, Joshua and many others had seen the angel of the Lord and had not died as a result. Others suggest that Gideon, like Isaiah and Job, was seized with a crushing awareness of his sinfulness as he stood bathed in this most terrible light of God. And now the angel was gone, and his sense of sinfulness remained. Left to his own devices, Gideon could have screamed himself across the precipice of madness within minutes.

Then that voice spoke again, but this time it came from inside his own mind. We will never know if he immediately realised and recognised the voice. Perhaps it spoke such good news that Gideon was tempted to wonder if the words were a product of his own wishful thinking, a vain effort by his imagination to calm the crushing fear.

'Shalom. Do not be afraid. You are not going to die.'

Relief flooded in, washing away the dark fear in a moment as surely as the fire had consumed the meal. God was good. God was kind. God was gracious. God was loving. God was for life. God is for me . . . God is . . . with Gideon.

Gideon spontaneously responded in gratitude, and, despite no order being given, as a love offering to God, he built an altar, and named it after the word that God had given: the Lord is peace.

As he knelt there and worshipped, he knelt by two reminders of the character of God that he would never be able to forget, even in moments of later sinfulness. The scorch that spoke of God's power, and the altar that spoke of God's peace. The mighty God and the gracious God, strength and kindness kissing. For a moment, we see the purpose of God for all of us – living in his shalom, in his peace. Shalom is the place of freedom, of justice and of our lives ordered according to God's purposes.

But if shalom is to be ours, it will surely flow out of a revelation of God that includes the white heat of awesome power and the softly spoken assurance of grace – the scorched rock and the altar of relieved gratitude. Christians become unbalanced when their concept and understanding of God is heavily weighted to emphasise one aspect of his nature at the expense of other aspects. We have all met the members of Scorched Rock Christian Centre. Eyes wide and ablaze with passion, their God trembles with billion-volt power. Their deity's favourite preoccupation is to toss deadly lightning bolts at the sinful and sincere alike. The members of Scorched Rock don't discuss or dialogue, they rant. Hell is more real to them than heaven. The angry God has been appeased through the shed blood of his Son, but only just. These people could do with a revelation of the child-kissing Christ, who abandoned an important summit meeting with the Pharisees in order to hand out hugs. They need a fifty-week sermon series on the father in the story of the Prodigal Son. Then they might be able to include a grace altar as part of their church furniture.

Then there are the laid-back, relaxed and utterly cool folks who attend the Shalom Community Church. Their God is more a mate than a Maker. Jesus is a thoroughly nice chap who wears an endless grin and whose fashion choice is usually a weary sheep, wrapped around his neck. Even the sheep grins blissfully. Jesus to them is a comfort, but not too much of a challenge. The Shalom crowd could probably do with an extended sermon series on the book of Hebrews and a few copies of *Sinners in the Hands of an Angry God* by Jonathan Edwards in their Christmas stockings. Donald McCullough asserts: 'It may well be that the worst sin of the church at the end of the twentieth century has been the trivialisation of God'[17], and invites his readers to heed the words of Annie Dillard

---

[17] Donald McCullough, *The Trivialisation of God* (NavPress, 1995)

Why do people in churches seem like cheerful, brainless tourists on a packaged tour of the Absolute? Does anyone have the foggiest idea what sort of power we so blithely invoke? The churches are children playing on the floor with their chemistry sets, mixing up a bunch of TNT to kill on a Sunday morning. It is madness to wear ladies' straw hats and velvet hats to church; we should all be wearing crash helmets. Ushers should issue life preservers and signal flares; they should lash us to our pews. For the sleeping god may wake some day and take offence, or the waking god may draw us out to where we can never return . . .[18]

It's difficult to balance the justice and mercy that are so perfectly entwined in the character of God. But the balance is critical lest we end up either in fear or flippancy. Under the oak in Ophrah, Gideon was perfectly aligned to the peace and purpose of God. Of course, that new order of God would now have to break out to the wider community – it was not for Gideon to keep and enjoy for himself. But that was for tomorrow.

---

[18] Annie Dillard, *Teaching a Stone to Talk* (Harper and Row, 1982), pp. 40–41

Chapter Five

Recovering Our Clarity

> Tear down your father's altar to Baal and cut down the
> Asherah pole beside it . . . build a proper kind of altar to
> the LORD your God . . . (Judg. 6:25,26)

Thirty hours had passed. Gideon sat bolt upright, his eyes
fixed and staring at the wall of his bed-chamber. His
eyes were reddened and ached now, the lids drooping and
heavy, but each time they closed, just for a moment, he
jolted awake again, his mind racing and alert. It had been a
frantic, sleepless night until the sun had climbed and
chased the cover of darkness away. And then, a long day of
mountain-top and valley emotions. Genuine exhilaration
one minute, as Gideon remembered that unforgettable
meeting and the thrill at the memory of the night's work for
God that followed. Then, without warning, in the midst of
delight, a dungeon door would slam on his heart, and there
in that cold place, icy bolts of fear stabbed at his heart. Now,
was it just a day later? Everything had changed, for ever.

The whirlwind thirty hours had begun at the altar of
gratitude. The Lord had spoken such a calming word of
peace, assuring Gideon that he would not die in an inciner-
ating ignition of judgement. And then, when at last the altar

was complete – a hastily built memorial to kindness – God had issued a command that required Gideon to risk the life that had just been spared. He must build another altar, not in the quietness of the remote winepress, but in the very heart of the town: in the Baal shrine, the contents of which he was told to demolish. This would strike a fatal blow to the Baal cult. It would be impossible for Gideon to lead a Yahweh-inspired battle campaign if the evil shrine in his father's satanic stronghold stood proud and unchallenged. That dark stain must first be cleansed from his home.

Gideon may well have been stunned at the command. His home was already a place of fear and threat. How would his father, the custodian of the shrine that he was about to destroy, respond to his son's treachery? And what would the reaction of the townsfolk be? They were passionately committed to Baal. But however deafening the shout of fear in his heart, the memory of the fire and the voice were more vivid. Gideon decided to obey, as long as he could do the work at night time. This was probably not to prevent reprisal. The dawn would reveal his handiwork soon enough, and, in a small town, it wouldn't take long to identify the culprit. The decision to carry out the mission under cover of darkness was probably made because the town was full of Baal loyalists, who would have physically prevented the operation during daylight.

It would be an awkward and back-breaking task, even with a strike team of eleven men. The Baal shrine was probably a huge, intimidating construction.[19] Gideon

---

[19] 'A Baal altar was found at Megiddo which measured some twenty-six feet across and four and a half feet high. Made of many stones, cemented together by mud, such an altar would constitute an immense task to destroy and carry away.' Leon Wood, *Distressing Days of the Judges* (Abingdon), p. 231

hastily summoned the household servants – as employees, they would presumably be the most trustworthy. Apparently there was no close-knit circle of friends for Gideon to call upon in his hour of need. His companions-in-arms would be hired helpers under orders, paid mercenaries rather than visionary crusaders. Gideon's mission was challenging, to say the least. The servants had to be organised – and there was, I suspect, always the risk that there might be a traitor in the midst who would defect and report the plan to Joash, or, worse still, sneak away in the darkness to gather a mob of townsfolk. The shrine could become a battleground. The demolition crew would then have to work in the straitjacket of silence. Perhaps two servants were dispatched to butcher the bull and backpack the joints of meat up to the high place. The others, Gideon taking the lead, tiptoed slowly through the sleeping town, scurrying from shadow to shadow. Once they were safely inside the shrine, the really difficult task began in earnest. The stones, welded together by old, flaking mud joints, were prised apart and perhaps carried one by one into the gloomy depths of the caves and discarded. Perhaps they ripped the Asherah pole out of the ground, and then carried it well inside the labyrinth of granite alleyways, where it could be safely hacked apart without fear of waking the town. The freshly chopped wood was then returned to the shrine. It would be put to good use in the construction of the much smaller altar to Yahweh. The mummified human heads were gently removed from the hideous swinging *teraphim*. Then, respect and restraint cast to the wind, the servants kicked and pummelled the clay figures to pieces, dry, powdery fragments flying everywhere. A furtive rush of joy coursed through them as they deliberately, scandalously blasphemed the Baal.

They followed Gideon's instructions with meticulous care, recycling the materials and building the new Yahweh altar. Just as the first hint of dawn edged the distant horizon, they laid the still warm and bloody parcels of meat upon the neatly piled wood. At last, a fire was made, and the shrine filled with smoke and the smell of wood and flesh burning. And then, while the township stirred, they climbed wearily down from the shrine, and scattered. It would not be long.

Perhaps it had been one of the elders of the town who had made the terrible discovery. He knew that something was very wrong when he passed the bull pen. The great bull, already reserved for the coming feast, stood alone now in a pen where two animals had stood the evening before. The other seven-year-old was gone. What was going on? It was not the Midianite way to slip into a town during the night to steal a single animal: they preferred the humiliation of daylight for their pillaging raids.

Minutes later, he stood, breathless now, at the entrance to the shrine. The walls echoed with every foul expletive he could muster, as he surveyed the scene before him. The smell of freshly turned earth and smoke filled his nostrils as he looked at the bare ground where altar stones had rested yesterday. The floor was littered with a thousand clay fragments; the incense holder shattered, hurled with great force against the far wall. But where was the precious pole? Had these wreckers taken that off into the night, a trophy to commemorate their night of wickedness? He kicked the charred carcass aside, and plucked a stray length of wood that had fallen out of the fire, and so had survived the heat. It was then that the horror of it dawned upon him – the Asherah pole had been used for this unsanctioned sacrifice. Cursing again, the man hurled the blackened length of wood back into the charcoal pile with violent force, scattering ash everywhere. Coughing and cursing still, the man picked his way down the rock face, and began to run, his voice angrily yelling the alarm.

Within an hour or so, an angry crowd had gathered. Religion is one cause that can so effortlessly rally a mob of fanatical avengers, particularly if unseen demons assume the role of cheerleaders. Accusation and recrimination boiled together on the streets; public order was beginning to break down. The city elders met hastily, went together to the shrine to view personally the shocking crime scene, and then convened a formal investigation. Who can know the agony that Gideon may have felt as he slid the great key into the lock of the house door, his ear pressed hard against the wood? He could hear the angry shouts in the street, an urgent chorus of chaos, the demands for blood to be shed, for the criminals to be found, for the harshest punishment to be meted out. Did he consider stepping out of the house, to make his way calmly through the crowd, presenting himself to the elders and, keeping his wavering voice as steady as he could, own up to the desecration? Was this his first day in the service of Yahweh and his last day on earth? When Yahweh had declared that he would not die, but live, did that assure him only that God would not kill him – or was he under divine protection from the baying crowd as well?

The inquiry continued. Many were publicly interrogated, and, at last, the crowd moved towards the old house where Joash and his son Gideon lived. Who knows where the incriminating evidence came from? Some writers, who believe that Gideon had been a lone witness for Yahweh for years before the winepress incident, suggest that, as a prophetic irritant in a Baal-obsessed community, the finger of suspicion would naturally point towards him. Others think that Gideon was finally identified because, in a small community, a secret shared with ten men won't stay a secret for very long. However the accused was named and the guilty verdict reached, it was not long before Gideon heard the distant shouts coming closer and the ominous marching feet of the approaching mob.

❅ ❅ ❅ ❅

Forgive me for putting it so, but it seems to me that God, in a sense, messed up Gideon's life. Admittedly, Gideon BW (Before Winepress) was not living in any kind of fulfilment, but he did at least have a fairly safe existence. Now, just a few hours after bumping into God, Gideon AW (After Winepress) is potentially a target for his father, his family, his fellow citizens and, of course, within a few more hours, the Midianites too. As we will see, they moved in quickly to try and quell what they saw as an emerging rebellion. So let's not think that God called Gideon to a quiet life. Indeed, the God who has a Son who does not 'come to bring peace, but a sword' (Mt. 10:34), invited him to step out, stand up and make a statement that spat in the face of his demonised culture. I believe that the church in the United Kingdom needs to hear a fresh challenge to break out and preach the gospel with bold clarity and warm compassion again.

I have been wrestling with the challenge to share Christ with people I meet – preaching about him to hundreds or thousands is just not enough. I've been examining my own life and history, to see if I am still willing to be a Gideon in my town.

My earliest days as a Christian were characterised by an evangelistic zeal that was obvious, uncouth and probably profoundly embarrassing. I sported a huge Christian badge, courtesy of my local Christian book-store, which screamed a subtle message for anyone I met: 'Hello, you're going to hell'. I turned every conver-sation – no, I *wrenched* every conversation – around to the subject of Jesus.

'Hello, Jeff, would you like a cheese sandwich?'

'No, thank you.' (Smiles smugly, and points finger skyward.) 'I have the bread of life.'

I was unwise, irritating, in-your-face and treated evangelism as an opportunity to say as many things about God as possible without pausing for breath. I shared Christ with a lot of people, and remarkably some came to faith as a result.

Then, somewhere along the line, I decided to become 'a little more mature'. Rejecting my earlier efforts as naïve and brutish, I swung wildly away from a con-frontational approach and decided to embrace a more laid-back, friendship-evangelism style. No longer did I want to offend anyone. No longer did I really want actu-ally to *say* anything about Jesus, preferring to show acts of kindness and hope that those on the receiving end would put two and two together and find that the equa-tion equalled God.

Lest I encourage yet another wild swing, let me say that I remain convinced that evangelism is best done naturally and relationally. There is a need for us to realise that evangelism can be a process as well as a crisis. We must preach the gospel with words, works and wonders. Information shouted about God is not enough.

But still I have been wondering: Am I living like a light? I was reminded of the late John Wimber's words: 'I never met a Christian until I was twenty-five – or at least, if I did, he was almost certainly undercover . . .'

Is it possible that we have lost sight of that issue called eternity, and the edge and urgency that the message conveys? In a reaction against 'pie in the sky' theology, with our emphasis on the kingdom being now, have we lost sight of the reality that we have a message that is bigger than life and death? Has the salt lost its savour?

Turn the light on, someone.

Gideon had to break out and put a very unsubtle axe to Baal's altar. Will our nation ever come to Christ if the messenger church is silent? Will there ever be revival if the signpost 'Church' is unreadable? Perhaps we need to allow the missionary God to 'mess up' our lives again.

❋   ❋   ❋   ❋

Gideon's mission: to live up to his name

When Gideon picked up an axe and swung it at the altar, he was doing, in a sense, that which he had been born for. As a member of the nation of Israel, he was called to live prophetically in the shalom of God: Israel was called to be a window through which the other nations could look to see God's character. And then, perhaps incidentally, Gideon's name means 'one who cuts down', and so the wild axe-wielding vandal reformer at the shrine was living up to that name. He was never ever created to hide – such an existence was unnatural. He was born to venture out with the dangerous God.

There is an erosion in our sense of identity as Christians when we, as those called to be followers of Jesus, stop sharing the good news of the gospel. First, the gospel itself contains such a strong mission imperative, and so if we truly 'believe' it, then we must share it. And to believe that people will suffer eternal separation from the love of God – however you specifically interpret the teaching of Scripture on hell – and then to be unconcerned about those going there, surely makes us more than just lazy Christians: we must be heartless monsters.

Perhaps that's why churches that place a low priority on evangelism end up as passionless, religious clubs, cheerleading on Sunday mornings about changing the world, but living in a kind of schizophrenia because we dust down our belief system on Sunday mornings – which includes heaven and hell – and then rub shoulders all week with those perhaps destined for the fire, but never take the time to mention what we say we believe. In that sense, I suggest that most of us Christians don't really believe in hell. As far as the New Testament is concerned, the reality of belief is always tested by action and fruit, and response to that belief. John rebukes those who say that they love God and still hate their brother. There's no mincing of his words – he calls us liars if we try to play that game. It has been said that 'that which we really believe, we live by – all the rest is religious froth'. Orthodox evangelicalism cannot be measured by our vague mental assent to a collection of doctrines. Christ demands not just filling our brains with his ideas, but the radical realignment of our lives in order to respond to the truth. Mission is not an option, a cause for the enthusiasts: it is a primary part of our new-found identity in Jesus.

Gideon's mission: to take the message out

Gideon was called to affirm in the marketplace that Yahweh was the Lord his God (Judg. 6:26). Private altars built in safe places are not enough for God. He wants his true followers to build more public, provocative testimonies. Such a challenge will, figuratively speaking, mess up our comfortable lives. It will open us to the possibility of being marginalised and ridiculed at best, and abused and persecuted at worst. Surely this is the only way that we can hope to see the demonic high places in our culture crumble and fall; as we are willing to be known as people who are marching to a different beat, and who are citizens of another kingdom. We too must break out and stand up again.

The early church is such an exciting model, because they were truly a church without walls. The unfolding story of the book of Acts is a saga of a dynamic, sent people, not locked behind closed doors enjoying God in their ghetto, but rather a people kicked out by the Spirit into the big bad world. The Holy Spirit came on the Day of Pentecost and clothed the trembling disciples with power. Within minutes, a newly-emboldened Peter throws the door of the upper room wide open and steps outside to explain to the gathering crowd that this is a move of God, not a raucous drinking party – after all, the bars were not open yet! Three thousand find Christ and are baptised. The church has firmly placed an axe in the marketplace.

Peter and John head for the temple to pray, but God does not want his works and power to be contained in the walls of that place, so a miracle occurs at the gate! By the end of Acts 3, the church is meeting in Solomon's court, a place in the outer extremities of the temple grounds, in the shadow of its east walls. The church was breaking out.

Within days, the city is buzzing with the story of the beggar who asked for a few coins and got his legs back. Persecution has begun in earnest, but the influence of the church is mushrooming. The sick are being healed in the streets.

The hum of persecution builds to a roar in the lynch mob-like execution of Stephen, but even this serves to push the church out further. In the scattering that followed Stephen's death, the Jerusalem-centred movement was catapulted into Judea and Samaria, and, because they gossiped the gospel as they went, the revival continued and grew. So it went on, including the cataclysmic conversion of the arch persecutor Saul, who would become an apostle to the Gentiles. Yet another wall collapses under the determined pressure of the gospel. The early church refused to throw a private party. Jesus had told them, literally, to be on their way (Mt. 28:19). They took his command seriously, and so it could be said of them that they filled Jerusalem with their doctrines (Acts 5:28).

So why is it that the church today is so contained in her special buildings and activities? It was Bishop William Temple who described the church as 'the only organisation that exists for the benefit of its non-members'. It's a snappy quote that is usually trawled out at just about every conference on the subject of mission and evangelism, but it's a theory that is seldom proved in practice. The church often exists only for the benefit of its members.

Consider the 'successful' church in America. Sixty per cent of the American population attend a church service once a month or more. There are incredibly beautiful and expensive church building complexes everywhere. On the surface, it's a strong church – so much so that once in Oklahoma, I was told (not too politely) 'Britain is spiritually barren. We are doing so well here. What's an Englishman like you doing over here? Why not take care of your own country?'

A reasonable question, to which I replied that despite the strength of religion, even Christian religion in the USA, America is still very much a mission field. Lifeless churches, that have a theology of an alive God but with a Sunday practice that advertises his possible death without a resurrection, abound. Despite the abundance of people who are willing to park their bodies in stained-glassed buildings week by week or month by month, society is still unravelling at an alarming speed. Children murder their teachers, politicians are expected to lie, and it seems that the church is somewhat walled-in. Ninety-five per cent of all evangelical Christians will never lead another person to Christ. The Assemblies of God is one of the more aggressively mission-centred denominations in the nation – and one of the larger groups too, with ten thousand churches in North America. But according to a relatively recent General Council report, one third of all Assembly churches did not see one single new convert in that year. In Britain it is no better. Many Christians have no meaningful friendship contact with non-Christians.

How could it be that the thrusting dynamic church that began with Acts is now so walled-in? Part of the problem goes back some 1,700 years, to a meeting held some time between AD 360 and 370. At Laodicea, a synod or church council met, and some cataclysmic decisions were taken, which are still giving us a hangover all these years later.

At Laodicea walls were formally erected between the so-called 'clergy' and 'laity'. The concept of eldership was replaced by priesthood. Up to Laodicea, the task of leadership was to equip the saints for the work of the ministry, as Ephesians 4 describes. After Laodicea, 'the ministry' became the exclusive domain of the paid professionals. A vast army was lost, marginalised.

At Laodicea, a decree was issued forbidding the cele-bration of the Eucharist, or communion, in a private home – formal rules about assembling together and for-mal seating arrangements were developed. Now a huge wall was built between the church and the community. The church gathering was taken out of the home next door – the 'go' was lost from the 'go and tell'. Now you had to go to a special 'sacred' building called 'a church' in order to hear the gospel.

Walls were built between men and women at Laodicea as well. It really was the most disastrous gath-ering. This same council banned women elders, and so in a stroke robbed women of the opportunity of leader-ship in the church.

The Lord's supper was no longer a significant, rela-tional meal, bursting with warmth and meaning. It had become enshrined in ritual and form. The church had moved from the home to the 'house of God'. The leaders were not just brothers and sisters, but priests set apart. And the original form of church was declared illegal.

Two thousand years later, we have millions of Christian books, Christian television and radio pumping the informational gospel twenty-four hours a day, and billions of pounds' worth of special buildings, but the reality is that much of the so-called 'work of God' goes on inside sacred walls, rather than out in the marketplace where it can do some good. We've even developed an extensive theology to justify our being apart from the world. We have a ghettoised doctrine of holiness, often quoting Paul's comment in 2 Corinthians 6:17: 'Therefore come out from them and be separate, says the Lord. Touch no unclean thing, and I will receive you.' This sounds as if we are justified in sitting in our nice build-ings and staying away from that big bad nasty world. Think again. God is calling us to a moral separation,

Jesus style. He was radically different from his grimy culture, but his was a resilient holiness that enabled him to rub shoulders with thieves and prostitutes and change their lives.

We have a ghettoised doctrine of buildings, when we refer to them as 'the house of God' or 'the sanctuary'. I will certainly not deny that you can sense an atmosphere of God in a lovely ancient building where the Lord has been exalted for hundreds or thousands of years, but the suggestion that the building is God's house infers that that's where he does most of his work. The building is meant as a headquarters for a mobile dynamic army, not a holy place for the elect to get away from the world eight times a week.

This 'church within walls' approach just doesn't work. One in every hundred converts comes as a result of a special crusade. The same number of converts come from visitation, and the same again have a crisis and call upon the church for help. Three in every hundred walk into a building and hear the message and respond, and the same again come to a special event. Five per cent come as a result of the ministry of Sunday school, six per cent as a result of activity by church leaders. So where do the rest come from? Eighty per cent come as a result of friendship. The heartbreaking thing is this: most Christians are so busy attending prayer meetings and being generally involved in the life of the church that they have no time to live out their faith in the marketplace. They are piously preoccupied, serving God in the winepress. If it weren't so tragic, it would be amusing. It's like a fisherman spreading his expensive net on the side of the riverbank, and then inviting the fish to jump out of the water and get caught.

Gideon had to get out there, and we have to as well.

Gideon's mission: to build up as well as break down

Gideon, wide-eyed with fear, stared across the room at his father. Joash sat very, very still, hands folded on his lap, seemingly oblivious to the scene of bedlam that was unfolding just outside his home. The crowd had reached a demonic screaming pitch now, and seemed only moments away from breaking the thick heavy door down. Kicking and punching at its panels, they roared out the demand. Gideon must be brought outside now. He was the guilty shrine robber. Punishment would be swift and bloody, as befitted the heinous crime.

Perhaps the strangest thought rushed through Joash's mind as he sat there, quiet, thoughtful, waiting. What was happening outside was a remarkable, vivid statement. The crowd had completely forgotten that he, Joash, was in charge of this town. It might well have been that their livelihoods depended solely upon him. Had they forgotten? Their fanatical allegiance to Baal was startling, even to the keeper of the Baal shrine. It was as if a group of Canaanites were outside the house now, not a band of Hebrews. Any sense of community or kinship had been destroyed by their Baal madness. Perhaps that was why Joash had not gone into one of his customary violent rages when his son confessed to the shrine business. It might have been that Gideon feared death at the hands of his own father. The crowd would be robbed of their prey, his father's hands tight at the throat of the son he had given life to. But the confession was met not with outrage, but with calm, with shame even, as if the sight of the rebuilt altar to Yahweh had stirred something in Joash that had lain dormant for years.

Slowly, unhurriedly, Joash stood up, and walked to the great door. Sliding back the bolt, and turning the key, he suddenly swung the door open. Immediately two or three men fell into the room, their shoulders having been at the door a second ago. They fell in an ungainly heap, and lay there, cursing and screaming.

And then the oaths died in their throats, as they looked up at Joash. It was one thing to be brave in absent fury, but quite another to stare the great man in the eyes and make your demands. A strange quiet fell upon the whole crowd. Joash was in no hurry, and made the most of the pregnant silence. The tension was tangible.

At last, Joash stepped across the threshold of the door, into the thick of the mob. Nervous, they stepped back, and now he stood, surrounded by them. He cleared his throat, and spoke, no hint of a waver in his voice.

'Are you going to plead Baal's cause? Are you trying to save him?'

He paused, and looked around, eyes piercing. The logic was brilliant: if Baal was alive, then let him fight his own battles. He doesn't need anyone to act on his behalf. Sensing that the mob understood, Joash added, thunder in his voice now: 'Whoever fights for him shall be put to death by morning! If Baal really is a god, then he can defend himself when someone breaks down his altar.'

The crowd were paralysed by the argument. If Baal was alive and well, then he would avenge himself. If he was dead, a non-god, a fraud, then it was all vain anyway, and Gideon deserved applause for delivering them of the myth.

They stood, quiet now, the rage of a minute ago a capped force. Joash had thrown every ounce of his authority behind the statement, threatening the execution of anyone who dared to cross him. And inside the house, Gideon looked at his father's square shoulders, and wondered.

❄   ❄   ❄   ❄

The first order of business for the newly commissioned Gideon and his crew was an act of demolition, but it is important to note that they were called to build a true altar to Yahweh as well. Their mission was first destruction, and then construction. Commentators have been quick to notice the apparent change of heart that took place in Joash when he faced the hostile crowd. Some have suggested that he was shamed by his son's bravery, but whatever the cause, the Baal custodian made a remarkable speech that suggested that his confidence in his dark religion had been diluted. It would appear that he had taken a number of steps towards the true God.

Gideon's act was far more than just the removal of paganism – it included the restoration of truth. His mission did not just pull down and wreck, it built up and established a new order, a new way of doing things.

I have often felt uncomfortable when walking by one of those brave gentlemen who stand out on the street corners and assault passing shoppers with King James Version Bible texts, normally verses about judgement and fire. The black gothic lettering on their placards screams the announcement of doom: repent or burn. It may be true, but is it a good news presentation? I recently heard of a young homosexual who was killed in a bar fight. A group of local 'Christians' decided to picket the funeral. Despite desperate begging by the young man's relatives, the 'believers' stood outside the cemetery, brandishing 'God hates queers' and 'Gays burn in hell' posters. Good news? I felt ashamed to even bear the name of Christian when I heard about their heartless, despicable behaviour.

Gideon's act was positive, and the evidence suggests that perhaps the hard-hearted Joash was moved somewhat as a result. When we share Christ with people, it will only be good news when we see them as being people God loves. People don't want to be considered the enemy at worst, and our targets or projects at best. That's why I find myself a little unnerved by the term 'friendship evangelism'. It sounds as if the Christians are cooking up a dastardly plot in order to reach the world by loving them, whereas people deserve love just for love's sake, regardless of whether they ever become Christians.

And sometimes, when the good news is good, they *do* decide for Christ.

❊　❊　❊　❊

For around seventeen years, I tried to get my father to become a Christian. I tried everything. I tried the blunt will-you-miss-the-abyss? approach: 'Hello, Dad. I am a Christian, and you, *sadly*, are not. You're going to hell. Have a nice day.' For some unknown reason, my father did not respond to this apocalyptic jabbing. I tried arguing with him, and often I was fairly successful at demolishing his objections. They crumbled to dust as I swung the sword of the Spirit, rattling off devastating scriptures like a machine gun. I certainly won a few arguments, but I didn't win my dad.

What I didn't realise then was that my father, a prisoner of war for four years during the last world war, had had a number of harrowing experiences that disabled his ability to believe in a loving God. He came to our church occasionally, listened patiently to my preaching, jousted with me in endless discussions and arguments, and steadfastly refused to make any moves towards God.

I was living in the USA when the breakthrough came. I was attending a conference where Korean pastor David Yongghi Cho, leader of the largest church in the world, was speaking. His talk that day was a passionate exhortation to trust God in prayer, particularly as we pray for relatives and friends to become Christians. At the conclusion of his talk, Cho ordered that the doors of the building be locked and commanded – literally – the few hundred leaders present to get on their knees and pray for people who didn't know Christ. My parents were coming to the USA for their first (and only) visit, and as my mother was already a Christian, I settled down and began to pray for my father. Within a few minutes, a picture began to form in my mind. It was of my dad, with tears running down his face. He was holding an open Bible in his hand. At first I was tempted to dismiss the vision as wishful thinking, but decided to accept it by faith. As I continued to pray, I felt an emerging confidence that my father would turn to Christ very soon.

They arrived four weeks later, at a little municipal airport in Southern Oregon. A large number of our friends went to the airport to meet them. I was astonished and somewhat embarrassed by the fact that our friends were holding little Union flags and posters that said, 'Welcome to America, Kath and Stan. We love you'.

My dad was delighted. During that month, he spent so much time talking that there weren't any donkeys with hind legs left in the entire state. Our friends listened, nodded and smiled, even though it was apparent that they didn't have a clue what he was talking about most of the time, because of his broad London accent. Most of all, our friends let my dad know that they were interested in him. They expressed love to him in a way that was truly humbling.

On his last Sunday in America, my dad became a Christian. He burst into tears at the back of a Sunday morning meeting – I don't think that I had ever seen him cry before. We walked to the 'altar' together as per the

American custom, and he turned his life over to God. The next evening, we went out for a meal to celebrate, and Kay and I handed him a new Bible, with his name engraved on the front. He opened the Bible, and a tear ran down his face, just as I had seen . . .

My father died a couple of years ago. I was asked to preach at his funeral, which was surely the most difficult sermon I have ever delivered. I decided to use his Bible, and so, when I was preparing, I looked through it to see if there were any notes that he had made. As I opened it, a book fell out, called 'How to know that you're a Christian'. It was one of those little books that are given out to people when they make a decision to follow Christ. I opened this booklet that I had never seen in his lifetime. There was a page of questions, and then pencilled writing where he had completed the work assignment. One of the questions was 'What was it that finally made you decide to become a Christian?' I took a deep breath as I looked down at his hasty scrawl. It was as I had suspected. After seventeen years of Bible-bashing and not-so-good news, it was love that broke through. My dad had written simply, *The love of my family and friends*.

❊　❊　❊　❊

Gideon could hardly believe it. The mob had become a crowd again; admittedly, some of them were still hot for blood to be shed, but even they had lost the sense of mad frenzy of just a few moments ago. It seemed that they were going to let the matter rest. The wisdom from a totally unexpected source – Joash – had triumphed.

Then one of them stepped forward and, for a moment, it looked as if he was going to dare to challenge the uneasy consensus.

'I have a proposal to make!' he yelled, and Gideon locked his facial muscles tight, desperate to show no fear. 'From now on, this man should be called Jerub-Baal. He wrestled with Baal, now let's see if Baal will come after him. He smashed up Baal's altar, now let's see what will become of him!'

If it was a ploy to place a curse upon Gideon, then it backfired. The new name, 'Baal-fighter', would catapult Gideon from obscurity to fame.

There was an immediate murmur of agreement. Within moments, the crowd, satisfied now, was gone. The door was shut, and the one who had been a dead man walking moments earlier returned to his bed-chamber. And once the door was closed, he began to laugh, his body racked with convulsions of joy. He didn't mind the new name at all. Baal might have a nasty reputation, but Gideon knew someone with a staff that shot fire and a voice that spoke peace. Let Baal contend with *him*.

Chapter Six

Clothed with God

> Then the Spirit of the LORD came upon Gideon, and he
> blew a trumpet . . . (Judg. 6:34)

Ophrah was buzzing with a mingling of excitement and
fear. In every home, the topic of conversation was the
same: the coming invasion. Word of mouth had reached
the town, confirmation of their nightmares – the
Midianites, together with their satanic allies, were in the
area once again. There was to be a robbery at harvest
time for the eighth successive year. And the rumours
were true. The enemy had already crossed over the
River Jordan, and now there was a massive encampment
in the Valley of Jezreel, at the eastern end of Esdraelon.
It was a favourite place for Midian, both for provision
and strategy. Jezreel was a very fertile region – the name
Jezreel means 'God sows' – and made an ideal base
camp for the raiding skirmishes that made Israel weep.
But amidst the rising terror, there was a heady, undis-
guised excitement. There was a new light in the eyes of
the older folk who could still remember Deborah. Was
this Jerub-Baal another like her? Certainly, the new altar
built for Yahweh had signalled a massive change in the

town. Now people were talking about Yahweh again, with honour and respect.

As for Baal – well, Jerub-Baal was still alive, wasn't he? If Baal was so powerful, why hadn't he acted in vengeance?

Was this really a new day that they were living in?

For the Midianites and their friends, it was business as usual – collection time, just as it had been for seven harvests previously. They were unaware that everything was, in fact, different. A man had met God, tasted his power and sensed his call. He had no impressive track record, and until recently had probably been completely unknown outside of his own community. But now the word was out, and behind cupped hands his name was spoken far and wide – the saga of the new Baal-fighter. As yet, there was no army to oppose Midian. There was no impressive storehouse of weapons; no generals scurried around a plan or a strategy. Just one man and God. Everything was indeed different.

※   ※   ※   ※

Where was Gideon when it happened; when the Spirit of God came upon him? Was he sitting alone in his home, fingers knotting and unknotting with anxiety as he pondered the task ahead? Was he out in the fields, walking and dreaming and talking animatedly to the God he now felt so intimately acquainted with? Or was he standing on the edge of a crowd, listening to the banter and the speculations and the stories, a mixture of faith and fear fighting within him as he listened? We don't really have any sense of what Gideon actually *felt* when the Spirit came. Did the experience begin with a sudden quickening of his heartbeat, or a liquid weight that seemed to be streaming down over his head, over his shoulders and down his chest? Was it a shocking surge of power, a bolt of energy that shot in an instant out of heaven? Or perhaps it was a quiet blossoming of peace that seemed to grow from deep inside of him, and then galvanised itself, solidified almost, so that Gideon felt that he was wearing a thick, impenetrable armour that no eye could see and only he could feel?

Scripture sums up the episode succinctly: 'Then the Spirit of the LORD came upon Gideon.' The Revised Standard Version potentially misleads us with the translation 'the Spirit . . . took possession', suggesting a violent encounter or invasion, as was to be the case with Samson (Judg. 14:6) and Saul (1 Sam. 11:6). Instead the Hebrew seems to suggest a very unusual experience. All the commentators agree that the language here suggests a 'special kind of incarnation', that God's Spirit put on Gideon's personality like a garment. This is not Gideon being clothed with God, but God clothing himself with Gideon, going deep within him and filling the very centre of who he was with the Spirit. David Jackman writes, 'We are told that the Holy Spirit put on Gideon like a suit of clothes, much as we might dress up for a special occasion, such as a wedding, or put on overalls to crawl under the car. Gideon is the clothing in which God is going to appear, the instrument that he is going to use . . .'[20]

Only two other biblical characters had the same experience: Amasai (1 Chr. 12:18), one of King David's generals who was clothed by the Spirit, and burst into a litany of encouragement and affirmation for David as a result; and then the unfortunate prophet Zechariah (2 Chr. 24:20), who, as a result of his encounter with the

---

[20] David Jackman, *Mastering the Old Testament – Judges, Ruth* (Word, 1993)

Spirit, prophesied just one message of judgement and was immediately stoned to death in the temple court as a result. Neither of these cases suggests a surge of strength or extraordinary physical power, but rather the ability to act in the wisdom of God. As Gideon moved forward in summoning the tribes and then going into battle, he was being directed by the Spirit of God within him. Jackman's analogy is helpful, too, in that it suggests the purpose of the clothing of the Spirit. He points out that the Greek word *dunamis* used in the New Testament has as its root meaning 'the ability to get the job done'. Some translations render the word 'enabling'. This is a vital point for us, particularly as we remember an infant church in the book of Acts filled with the same Spirit on the Day of Pentecost. The Spirit came as they were poised on the springboard of mission, granting them an undeniable experience – not an experience for the sake of itself, but to help them to get the job done in Jerusalem, Judea, Samaria and the uttermost parts of the Earth. The Spirit enables Gideon. The Spirit enables the New Testament church. Perhaps as we adjust our priorities and regain a mission focus, we will know more the Spirit who comes, not just to give us goosebumps, but to empower us for service.

The fog that had been swirling around in Gideon's mind suddenly cleared. He too had heard that the Midianites were mustering, and this time it was a huge army camped out there at Jezreel, rumoured to be in excess of a hundred thousand men. But in his heart, where fear had frozen his soul previously, the warmth of hope now seemed to live. It was not that God had *said* anything more to him, rather that everything had changed because, remarkably, the God who had been *out there* now seemed to be *within him*. And there was a sudden certainty about his next step. He would have to issue a call to arms, just as Judge Ehud had done before him (Judg. 3:27). He would take the *shophar*, the ram's horn, to his lips, fill his lungs with air and give a two-tone blast. The high, shrill sound would be heard at a great distance. The only question was, where would he start? Whom would he call? Immediately a door of understanding opened in his heart and mind, and he knew. He should do as he had done before, with the dark shrine. He should start at home.

※　※　※　※

Despite his developing fame, Gideon was still faced with a formidable challenge: how could he convince the nation that they should stand up and fight their oppressors? These were the people who had impotently allowed themselves to be plundered for seven long years, years that had pulverised their confidence and smashed their identity. It was one thing for Gideon to take a brave step to restore the altar of Yahweh in his own small town, but quite another to lead a nation into battle. How do you get from the place of obscurity to the platform of influence?

Anyone who has ever aspired to serve God has felt the same challenge. Stirred by the Spirit, head full of dreams, we desperately want to make a difference for the King and the kingdom, but how do we get from where we are to where we sense that God wants us to be? I have been approached so many times by people who really want to preach and teach. Some, admittedly, watch the preacher at work, see their ability to win a crowd and perhaps are thrilled with the 'glamour' of itinerant ministry or international travel. Most, however, have earnestly and sincerely sought the face of God, and have become convinced that this is what God has called them to do. But where to now? Is there a model for the development of ministry in the local church and beyond?

This is a vital issue. I have spoken in some churches that were being torn apart by 'people with a ministry'. I have become convinced that teaching people 'how to discover their gifts' – an important subject – is irresponsible if we are not willing to teach them how to see those gifts develop and emerge properly and appropriately. Consider, for example, the church where the gifts of the Spirit are regularly in use, and the well-worn phrase 'God told me' frequently appears in everyday conversation. As a result of a very genuine climate of enthusiasm in the church, suddenly there are people popping up everywhere announcing with fervent zeal that 'God has given them a ministry'. One has just returned from a conference on deliverance and, as a result, has determined that they are the God-appointed Witchfinder General for the local church. Binding and loosing just about everything that moves, they roam the church on a demon safari, and damage a lot of innocent people as they go. Another had a dream in the night during which an obscure but impressive angel announced that they were to lead worship with songs 'which the Lord is going to give me'. Fearing that we will quench the Spirit, we unleash the budding Kendrick the following Sunday, and conclude that the Lord gave them those songs because he didn't want them. I once met a man who is destined to be the next President of the United States of America. He is a logger by trade, has no political experience or knowledge whatsoever, and has made no attempt to take any steps towards a career in politics; he will go straight from the woods to the White House. God has told him so . . .

Territorialism can creep into ministry as well. I have been to so many churches where just one look at the pianist suggested that they have erected a barbed wire entanglement around their keyboard. The playing of the pianoforte has become *their ministry*. Touch their ministry, and they will break your face. Suggest that someone else play next Sunday, and World War Three will break out.

Believe me, misdirected enthusiasm and gift recognition without a context can damage churches beyond repair. So is there an appropriate pattern for the development of ministry? Gideon can help us.

❊　❊　❊　❊

Read the story of Gideon carefully, and you discover the God who develops people. Gently, graciously, with tender kindness and confirmation – and sometimes even by responding to what may have been blatantly sinful prayers – God nurses Gideon forward into usefulness. The call of Gideon is a process as well as an event; a journey as well as a crisis.

The same is true when Gideon begins his public ministry as a judge/deliverer of Israel. A three-step programme of development can be clearly seen as Gideon takes the rallying trumpet to his lips, and prepares for battle.

First of all, Gideon's influence and ministry gradually *emerge*. He does not take the giant leap from the winepress to the nation overnight. They emerge first in the assault on the Baal altar – an event which serves as a workshop for Gideon's faith development – and then as he plays the battle trumpet to his own family members. The shrill notes are first heard by 'Abiezer', which is Gideon's family name. His new reputation as a Baal-fighter was best known by his family members. Would they respond to the trumpet call?

They did and so, encouraged by that, Gideon then took his musical summons to the rest of the tribe of Manasseh, who were also willing to dance to his tune. Courage rising, he gave a further call, probably by herald, to the tribes of Asher, Zebulun and Naphtali. All four of the tribes that Gideon called came from the Esdraelon Plain, and therefore were the tribes most hurt by the inroads of the Midianites. They would be quick to respond to the battle call.

Gideon does not stomp on to a platform of prominence; rather there is a progressive emerging of his gift as judge, first in his own locality, and then further afield. The analogy is obvious but useful. Those who will aspire to significant service – and let's never lose sight of the reality that all ministry is a call to servanthood, not glory – must first be willing to be faithful in the small, supposedly insignificant details of life. I now have the privilege of addressing tens of thousands of people every year as I travel to preach and teach, but that platform was not built overnight. I recall that as a younger leader, I experienced feelings of great frustration because I had little opportunity of influence for God at a broader level than the little church that I led. I particularly remember walking along a beach, and complaining to God about my limited sphere of ministry. God whispered a question that day, a question that became an answer and halted my complaining. He simply said,

'Would you like to step on to a platform that I have not lit for you?'

Let your gifting gradually emerge. By all means talk to leaders about your burdens and aspirations, and seek opportunities to develop your gift – those who feel a call to preach need to preach! But appointment to leadership is not the bestowing of a title in the hope that God will then bestow a gifting to match the title; rather it is the recognition of that which God has already bestowed.

That's what happened for Gideon. First his family and friends, then his tribe and then others began to arrive. They saw and sensed the hand of God upon his life, and in so doing *recognised* his gift. Simplistic though it sounds, Gideon was a leader because people were willing to follow him, even into a battle where they were massively outnumbered and had the most bizarre weapons. Leaders can protest that they are called to lead as much as they like, but if no one around them recognises that and starts to follow, then they are in major difficulty!

If God hasn't given the gift of leadership, then training, ordination and using impressive credentials and titles won't create leadership. As the hundreds and the thousands began to gather, Gideon knew once and for all that this was no game. Battle was imminent; this was for real. Feeling that things were racing at a pace beyond his control, despite being filled with the Spirit and surrounded by a gathering army that only reinforced and confirmed his calling and gifting, Gideon was on the brink of yet another crisis.

❊   ❊   ❊   ❊

Maybe the thought had hit him in the middle of a hot, sleepless night, when sleep evaded him and death lingered in the shadows of his room. The sweaty night may have come at the end of a day of public bravado, hugging and backslapping and big talk of battles to come, but behind his certain grin and his speeches hesitation nagged: the size of the challenge ahead was overwhelming. The gathered army was sizeable, but would be outnumbered by four to one on the battlefield. Their weapons were non-existent – previous raids by the oppressors had probably emptied any secret armouries. And so, not surprisingly, morale was low. The crowds had responded to the summons, but brave hearts were few. The air was thick with an ominous sense of gloom. The more days that passed, the more distant was the memory of the winepress fire and the voice of peace. The threat of a cold, bloody sword driven through his heart was more real and vivid now. We can all be armchair radicals, fantasising about great, imaginary exploits. But when the bell tolls for battle, and the fantasy has to become reality, courage can easily waver.

Hence the now famous fleece. It would appear that Gideon was becoming a sign addict, needing more and more assurance as the day of battle hastened. He proposes another test to God, which some commentators describe as little more than a trick. It is a simple 'if such and such happens, then that would mean such and such' routine. Gideon will place a whole fleece – not a few wisps of wool – upon the threshing floor. If, in the morning, there is dew on the wool but the ground is dry, then this will mean that God is truly with Gideon, and battle can commence. God obliges, and the bleary-eyed, reluctant Gideon squeezes out a bucketful of water from the fleece. He is forced to conclude that it's time for war.

Until Gideon comes up with another twist. This time, he will ask God to make sure that the fleece is *dry* while the ground is wet. Think about it: this would truly be a miracle. The first test was not that conclusive as it would be usual for the ground to dry first, with moisture remaining in the fleece, but for the fleece to dry before the ground . . . Now that *would* be a sign from God.

Commentators have speculated endlessly about the significance of the dew in the test, reminding us that dew is a sign of provision given (Gen. 27:28) or withheld

(Gen. 27:39). Dew was considered to be a sign of security, prosperity and salvation – in short, of shalom. Perhaps Gideon was looking for a further sign of shalom, the altar being a fading memory.

The real issue of interest is: was Gideon right to do this? Read through enough books on guidance and you'll know that the practice of 'putting out a fleece' has at least been fairly common when it comes to decision-making. Again, the scholars are divided: some bluntly brand the fleece episode as 'Gideon's sin', while others are more kind: 'We ought not to blame Gideon for putting out his famous fleece . . . here the Lord is coaxing along a reluctant leader who really is diffident, modest and shy, and who needs to have his confidence built up step by step by a patient, loving, but determined God.'[21]

Perhaps both are right. Fleece-laying is generally not good practice – that much is certain from Gideon's own words. He apologises to God even as he puts in his request, and asks the Lord not to be angry with him as he plays this fleece game. He seems to know himself that this is not his greatest moment. He is asking for God to repeat what has already been spoken and confirmed by fire and peace. The sign has nothing to do with the issue in hand, that of fighting a battle. In playing the fleece game, Gideon ignores the gathered thirty-two thousand men – a real sign that relates to battle – and turns his attention instead to a rug. And then he is not true to his word. When the first test is fulfilled, he decides that he is not satisfied, and asks for a reversal of the test and therefore another sign.

Some see something more sinister at the threshing floor. They sense the possibility that Gideon is now

---

[21] Michael Wilcock, *The Message of Judges – the Bible speaks today series* (Leicester: IVP, 1992)

yielding to fear, and so is trying to manoeuvre his way out of having to obey God's command and call: 'Gideon was not really seeking to know the nature of God's will, but to have that will changed. He simply felt that the problems were too great to proceed, and therefore, what God had previously said must somehow be wrong . . .'[22]

It is possible to play that game – laying a ridiculous fleece as an attempt to escape obedience. 'Lord, I will start tithing if . . . if I win the lottery today . . . even though I don't buy lottery tickets . . . Amen.'

Some Christians do get into this 'circumstantial what-if' routine. Bear in mind that Gideon was asking, in the second test, for a miracle, not just a confirming circumstance. How many of us have prayed the 'if the next traffic light is green then I will be a missionary' game, only to slow down when we see the distant green light and proceed only when the light is red, and thus discard the missionary call? Such games of chance are foolish.

My conclusion is that 'laying a fleece' is not the greatest idea. And, of course, my conclusion is wrecked by the fact that I, together with many other Christians, have known God speak to me as I 'laid a fleece', particularly in my earlier years as a Christian when I didn't know any better. Perhaps that's the reason why God was so kind in answering Gideon, even though the method of asking was flawed. The fact that God heeded Gideon's request doesn't mean that God approved of Gideon's approach.

What is proven is that the God whom we serve is a loving, compassionate Father who knows that we are fragile and weak yet still determines to hear our faulty prayers and enjoy our imperfect, tinny worship. As

---

[22] Professor Leon Wood, *Distressing Days of the Judges* (Zondervan/Academic, 1975), p. 213.

Gideon emerges into ministry, we see the surprising sight of a man full of the Holy Spirit, who still has doubts. It's a comforting sight, and teaches us that even the power of God doesn't overrule our personality and instantly remove our weakness. What is even more remarkable is the vision of a God who heard a bleating from the threshing floor, and who, out of grace and love, decided to help his worried servant out. Now that's a God worth going into battle for. Armed with a souvenir fleece, Gideon was about to do just that.

But not before God unveiled a few more surprises . . .

Chapter Seven

Less Is More

The LORD said to Gideon, 'You have too many men'
(Judg. 7:2)

The sun had only just begun its morning climb, but the fading shadows around the beautiful spring of Harod were being chased away quickly. In the half light, Gideon surveyed the huge Midianite encampment in the plain below. Israel was camped on the steep, bare slopes of Mount Gilboa. He looked across the plain at the hill of Moreh, which was just three miles to the north-west. Even that had groups of Midianites camped around its western flank, their countless camels tethered together. Shielding his eyes against the strengthening sun, he watched them, wondering at the sheer enormity of their forces. Once again, the analogy of locusts came to mind. Teeming, ravenous, hungry locusts. Even though he had heard the intelligence reports about the numbers of enemy troops, it was still something of a surprise actually to see their massive encampment. And then he had the strangest thought: this huge force would know that he and his army were there at Harod, 'the fountain of trembling'. They were probably watching him as he watched them. He realised that they would be uncon-cerned, knowing that they outnumbered his forces by nearly four to one.

Enough. Pondering the size of the challenge only served to dilute his courage. As he ran quickly back to his own camp, he considered what to say to his men. Harod was living up to its name: the expressions on the faces of the makeshift Israelite army did not radiate con-fidence or calm. They were terrified. Perhaps God would grant Gideon wisdom to calm their fears . . .

Should he tell them the story of the winepress just one more time, or were they becoming weary of it now? And what about the dew on the threshing floor? It was real enough to him, but seemed somehow vague and dis-connected in the telling. He needed something to stir them, to calm them. Like the restless stamping of the camels in the valley below, his men were taut with anx-iety. In recent hours their fearful imaginations had forced them to stare into the grim face of death; agonis-ing, violent death; children without weapons on a bloody battlefield, lambs to the Midianite slaughter.

The familiar voice within surfaced, and he laughed at the power of fear. His mind was playing tricks now, dis-torting even the voice that he had come to trust. The voice spoke again, stronger, surer now, yet still it spoke the same mad, suicidal message. There it was again, a silent shout in his soul, demanding a response: *'You have too many men.'*

❊   ❊   ❊   ❊

Put yourself in Gideon's shoes. You're scared, tired, uncertain – and outnumbered by nearly four to one. Your army can easily be outrun, because you don't have any camels. They are walking targets, because you don't have any weapons to speak of. They are understandably terrified. It's appropriate that they're camping at a place called 'Trembling'. You long for some of that wisdom God has been supplying.

His answer comes in the form of a command radically to reduce your manpower. You are to invite any who are scared simply to return home. Admittedly, this was a practice commanded in the Law, whether or not Gideon was aware of it. Moses had commanded that the faint-hearted should be invited to leave a battlefield before hostilities began (Deut. 20:8). Nonetheless, this was hardly the strategy that Gideon wanted to hear. He needed assurance and comfort when he had thirty-two thousand troops. Imagine how his heart sank when twenty-two thousand of those declared a sense of nervousness and went home! Now they were outnumbered thirteen to one by the cursed Midianites. Who knows how the ten thousand felt as the twenty-two thousand walked away, back to homes and families and relative safety, back home with the branding that fear had made cowards of them, but back home nonetheless?

Did Gideon wonder if he had finally toppled over the precipice of insanity when the voice spoke again? *'There are still too many men.'*

These ravings, these delusions would be the death of them all, or the saving of them, if this was the voice . . .

Apparently God wanted to sift the remaining ten thousand. The Hebrew means 'to sort them out', as a goldsmith sorts pure metal from dross. The test for the sifting appears bizarre: it centred around the method of drinking that the thirsty soldiers would employ. There would be those who would kneel to quench their thirst, and those who would remain standing, stooping down to scoop water up in their hands. God's verdict was simple: send home those who knelt down! I cannot imagine anything other than screaming panic swirling through Gideon's mind as he watched another 9,700 of his troops be disqualified. Leaving their jars and supplies with the hapless three hundred who remained, they walked back to their tents, away from the fight to come, relieved perhaps, possibly confused at the strange warrior's test. Add it up. Gideon's army was now outnumbered to a ratio of four hundred to one. The odds were absolutely, totally impossible. And God smiled. There was room for him to work now.

❋   ❋   ❋   ❋

This was a harrowing time for Gideon, but serves as a mine of information for us as we consider some important questions. How can we know the victory of God in our own lives? What kind of person does God choose to fight in his army?

Weakness is strength

The key to the strategy of reduction is found in the statement of explanation that God graciously gave to Gideon. He sent crowds of men off the field of battle 'In order that Israel may not boast against me that her own strength has saved her' (Judg. 7:2). If the whole of Gideon's army had remained, and they had won the battle with God's help, they would have been tempted to think that *they* were the heroes – pride would rush in. As it turned out, Israel would be quick to forget God's involvement in this miracle battle. Later, when offering the triumphant Gideon the kingship, they would declare that *Gideon* had saved them in battle, with no mention of Gideon's God (Judg. 8:22). Pride has a short memory, and an incredible ability to drive us to exalt ourselves. Odds of four to one, and thirteen to one, were not long enough to ensure that Israel would give credit to God. Only when the odds were lengthened to the impossible four hundred to one was there assurance that Israel would be certain that God had helped them, and that victory was not due to their own tactical brilliance! It should come as no surprise that the prophetic voices in our own day are calling the church to humble herself before God. Pride is a dangerous killer on the battlefield.

Many years later, a man called Paul would write in honour of his own weakness, having realised that his weakness was the ideal arena for God to work. His assertion that 'when I am weak, I am strong' is no happy-clappy cliché, but the verdict of a man who knew how to be self-sufficient and independently proficient, and who had then known the depths of despair and disappointment. His conclusion was that God tended to show up more when he was weak. Gideon's army would go to battle with a secret weapon that was completely unknown to the Midianites and their allies. They would depend upon the God of the universe.

❉　　❉　　❉　　❉

'I have a prophetic word that I want to give you, but I'd like to do it publicly during the meeting tonight.'

I've already mentioned that I tend to collect words from the Lord wherever I go. However, this was Gerald Coates speaking. I work alongside Gerald as part of the Pioneer Team, and I am very familiar with his prophetic ministry, which is uncannily accurate. I was intrigued, excited and hopeful that God was going to say something encouraging to me through Gerald. I was feeling in need of encouragement, having met my fair share of

'I want to tell you something in love, brother' Christians over the preceding months. I love to use humour when I speak. Most people like to laugh, and some (who make me decidedly nervous) apparently hate to laugh. Having been told off a few times, I had complained to God, and asked a question: 'Lord, have you called me to be a fool for Christ?'

The answer was simple, resounding and didn't please me at all. 'Yes.'

So, with that in mind, I had attended the Pioneer leaders' conference, smiled at my friends, but inwardly was feeling rather battle-weary and not a little bored with being a fool.

That evening Gerald preached, and at the conclusion of his talk he invited me to step up on to the platform. Nine hundred leaders leaned forward, interested to see and hear what would happen next. Gerald produced a jester's cap – multi-coloured, complete with little tinkling bells – and placed it upon my head. I was immediately angry. Some of the nine hundred started to laugh. I really did look very stupid. Others, more pastorally sensitive types, were reluctant to join in with the mirth, but that concern didn't last long. Within seconds the place was reverberating with laughter, and I was very, very angry. How dare Gerald humiliate me in this way? What was he playing at, sticking this ridiculous hat on my head in front of all of these people? And then he began to prophesy. The laughter faded, my anger died and the tears started.

'You have been willing to be a fool for Christ.'

Gerald had no knowledge of what God had said to me about my calling as 'a fool'. This was God! He then began to prophesy about a new season in my life, when the anointing of God would be stronger, when criticism would come thick and fast. He spoke of a need for me to learn to lean, to depend more and more upon Jesus every day. Anointing, criticism and dependency. He then presented me with a bishop's staff, a genuine antique (it used to belong to Bishop Trevor Huddleston) which had ended up in the hands of my colleague and friend Roger Ellis. Gerald took the staff from Roger, and placed it in my hands. Of course, it wasn't Gerald's to give, but he's like that!

'Carry this staff wherever you go in ministry, as a reminder to you that you *must* depend upon God . . .'

That staff went with me for many, many miles. It was with me when I spoke at interdenominational retreats; in Baptist, Anglican, Pentecostal and newer churches; it criss-crossed backwards and forwards across the Atlantic more times than I care to remember. Almost every time I flew internationally, the staff was either lost in the baggage hold or delayed and I was left waiting in the airport, the last person in baggage reclaim, while they found the thing. It was big and cumbersome. I travelled to a meeting by train once, and as I got on to the train, I accidentally swung the staff and hit a fellow passenger on the ear. I apologised profusely, and he gave me a look that suggested that I would do well to seek psychiatric assistance. I didn't know what to say. 'Sorry, friend, but it's a prophetic thing . . .'

I took the staff to Spring Harvest, and carried it on to the Big Top platform and around the site, from seminar to seminar. One helpful chap suggested that I might want to discard it in favour of a staff-shaped lapel pin. I laughed, and then responded with a smile: 'The reason that I'm carrying this big, inconvenient piece of furniture is simple. I need something big enough to mess up my life, delay me and get in my way so that I will not forget my need to lean upon Jesus – to depend fully on him every day of my life.'

Then an airline decided to go one better and instead of just mislaying the staff, they lost it completely. But when I consider the disabling power of pride in Gideon's story, and just how easy it is for us to rely upon ourselves, I begin to think that maybe I should have another wooden reminder for the rest of my days.

❋ ❋ ❋ ❋

Attitude matters

The 'reduction' strategy dealt a death-blow to the root of potential arrogance, but there was also a tactical reason for sending the first twenty-two thousand soldiers home. God doesn't play tricks with us. There is always method in what may appear to be his madness. The Law spelt it out: 'Then the officers shall add, "Is any man afraid or faint-hearted? Let him go home *so that his brothers will not become disheartened too.*" ' (Deut. 20:8, italics mine). Any military tactician will confirm that good morale is vitally important for any army. Whatever their strategic skills and technical proficiency, an army with a broken heart is destined to lose. Fear and negativity are so contagious; therefore it was important to make sure that only those with a positive attitude remained to fight, lest the battle be lost before it began. The Promised Land eluded a weary group of wilderness trekkers because they chose to believe the negative report of the ten returning spies. They were beaten without a weapon ever being lifted in anger; paralysed by pessimism (Num. 13:32).

Why is it that there are some people in church life who seem to love the negatives? Like hippos wallowing in delicious, filthy muck, they thrive on hassle and confrontation, grabbing at every issue and cause that floats by them, always ready for another crusade. To them, issues matter more than people. Any amount of time spent around these folks is draining and demotivating: they ultimately alienate even their closest friends. Leaders dread the sight of them. Perhaps the tactic of sending the twenty-two thousand home seemed like madness, but it was a blessed reduction. They would have been a liability on the battlefield, and ultimately their attitude would have made them a weapon in the hands of their enemies.

Ready and willing

Two-thirds of the original army were dismissed on the basis of attitude, and then 97 per cent of the remainder were sent back to their tents because they failed the 'sip' test at the spring. Was this simply a means of further reduction, or was there any reasoning behind the procedure?

Commentators have performed all kinds of acrobatics in order to make sense of this passage. Some suggest the possibility of leeches in the water, and so those who lifted water in their hands were more prudent. Others suggest that Gideon only ever intended to use a small commando unit, and the water test was an ingenious method of reducing his numbers without offending any of his now bold and willing warriors.

The heart of the matter is this: God made the announcement that there were still too many. God initiated the strange test: I will sift them. God became the coach who picked his own team: 'If I say this one shall go, he shall go, but if I say this one shall not go, he shall not go . . .'

It's possible that the test was designed to test the character of the soldiers. Those who knelt on the bank and just drank greedily would render themselves vulnerable to sudden attack, their watchfulness and alertness temporarily suspended by their own personal needs. Those who stooped and collected small amounts of water in the cupped hands, lapping it like a dog, would be able to keep watchful and ready even as they drank. If the test meant anything, it seems likely that God was looking for those who were alert and available as opposed to those preoccupied with their own comfort. Then the bad news: 9,700 were disqualified.

I wonder how that would compare statistically with a survey of those serving God today? Is it possible that we too have a vast army of people who are happy to come to feeding time on Sundays, and even sing stirring battle songs in the stained-glass greenhouse of the church building, but when it comes to aligning their priorities with those of the King are just too busy for battle? Gideon's experience shows us that God uses people who make themselves willing and available to him. The call of the prophet Isaiah teaches us this too. As far as I know, there was only God, Isaiah and some attending angels around when Isaiah had his 'Woe is me, I am unclean' crisis. The Lord kindly despatched an angel to take a hot coal and burn the man's mouth as a helpful(?) sign that he had been forgiven. Then the Lord dropped what appears to be a cosmic hint, booming out, 'Whom shall I send? And who will go for us?' Pause there. There's only Isaiah in the picture. Apparently God is hunting for volunteers. Getting the big hint, Isaiah responds, 'Here I am, Lord, send me.'

Get the hint?

※　※　※　※

How did the three hundred feel, as they said goodbye to their retreating brothers? Were there those who cursed what they thought was bad luck, in the way that they had passed – or failed – the test? Were there men who headed back to their tents angry and bitter because they had been eager for Midianite blood, had lived for many days in anticipation of the moment when a ravaged daughter could be avenged, a ruined crop paid for with a life? Had they passed the trembling test, only to fall at this hurdle? And did any of those who remained yearn to change places with those who quickly walked away now? As they said their goodbyes and collected all the provisions and the trumpets from those who would not be fighting now, did they feel as if they were bidding friends farewell for ever, such was the suicidal nature of their mission?

Three hundred against one hundred and thirty-five thousand.

Four hundred of Midian for every one of Israel.

Chapter Eight

Dancing in the Dark

Nothing great was ever done without much enduring.
(Catherine of Sienna)

Gideon was no longer simply afraid; now he was very afraid. Looking down at the huge, teeming army below in the valley and looking back at his own motley crew of three hundred only made him more anxious. It was probably late evening when God came again, kindness personified.

The full moon fell across Purah's face, his eyes widening as Gideon recounted what God had said. It was time to go into battle: God was going to give the enemy camp into Gideon's hands. There was an unusual contingency that God had provided. It was an invitation rather than a direct command. If Gideon was needing further reassurance, then he should go down to the Midianite outposts, where he would find encouragement from the most unusual source: the whispered conversations of the sentries. Notice again that God offered Gideon the opportunity to make use of this provision, or not, according to the level of his fear.

As silently as possible, Gideon and Purah crept down the rough slope. With every crouching step they took, the Midianite camp seemed to grow larger, and as they descended into the valley, it seemed totally to dominate the horizon. Gideon was coming face to face with his fear. The outposts were normally manned by the main striking forces of the Midianite hordes – the raiders who would fan out and plunder and pillage and then return to base camp. These elite groups, better disciplined and more heavily armed, were usually deployed around the perimeters of an encampment in order to provide the maximum protection and security.

Inch by inch now, they continued their painstaking descent and approach and, soon enough, they paused, pressing themselves hard into the earth, catching the first hint of voices on the gentle wind. Slowly, silently now . . . don't disturb any loose stones on the slope. Even your breathing sounds deafening. You purse your lips and breathe through the nose and hope and pray that they can't hear the hammer of your heart thundering in your chest . . . and then the muffled murmur of conversation in the distance begins to clear, and you can make out just a few words. What words from the lips of a Midianite could encourage them? God had only said that Gideon would be encouraged by what he would hear – no more advance detail was given.

It was one of those last-thing-at-night conversations when tiredness loosens the tongue and personal reflections tumble out more easily. One of the sentries had evidently dreamed a puzzling, frightening dream, the details of which obviously alarmed him. Doom in his voice, he told of the strange vision of a Midianite tent – probably the Midianite chieftain's tent – being flattened by a huge, rolling loaf of barley bread. It was certainly a bizarre picture. Great significance was attached to dreams in those ancient times, especially if the dreamer held some rank or authority. An interpretation would be anticipated and, sure enough, the other sentry immediately unlocked the rather obvious riddle. The loaf of bread was a well-known symbol of Israel, a symbol despised among the nations. The barley loaf was only eaten by the poorer classes, and Israel had been crushed economically by the Midianites, becoming a nation of slaves to their whims. But now that humble loaf was rolling relentlessly towards the Midianite tent – and to the nomad, the tent was his life. The nomadic tribes would look down with disdain upon the settled town dwellers – for them, the tent was the centre of everything. Now that tent, their very way of life, was going to be crushed and flattened by an uprising of poor, humble Hebrews. If only the Midianites had known the truth, that just a few hundred lay in wait at the place of trembling. Instead, they worried and fretted, because God had planted terror in the camp.

It was an elaborate set up, this dream episode. God carefully steered Gideon to the right section of outposts, and having dropped a nightmare into a snoozing sentry's mind, God then made sure that Gideon and his servant arrived just as the dream was being shared, and the interpretation was being given. Now, not only had the prophetic promise been confirmed once again by a Midianite-turned-prophet under the sovereign hand of God, but Gideon was also able to report back to his troops that the Midianites were in a state of fearful panic. God set it all up because, in order to fight, Gideon needed first to be encouraged or, as one version puts it, 'his hands were strengthened'. Gideon was afraid and in the dark, so God went to some rather elaborate lengths to provide an opportunity to build him up.

Pause for a moment. Dancing in the dark isn't easy. We all need those sources of strength that keep us going when things are tough and the battle is hard. For

Gideon, encouragement began before he ever overheard the prophetic dream. God specifically commanded that he take his faithful servant and armour-bearer Purah along for the reconnaissance trip. Obviously this was for protection, should they stumble into an outpost, but perhaps there was another deliberate reason for Purah to go along. Every other revelation of God had come to Gideon when he was alone, be it the outward manifestations of fire or the inner prompting of that voice. Now it would be good for the final comfort and confirmation to be revealed before a witness. Gideon would not be able to shake his head and wonder about the delusions that come in the night. Purah was there. He saw, he heard, he would remember.

God has not intended that we walk through the darkness alone. Years ago we sang a lilting song: 'He is all I need, he is all I need, Jesus is all I need'. Lilting indeed, but theologically bankrupt, because Jesus has not created me with a need only for him. I need the warmth and friendship and love and laughter that only friends can bring. That's one of the primary reasons that God gave us church – not so that we might sit facing the same direction, engaging in the weekly corporate rituals, but that we might walk through dark times together, weeping with those who weep, a prophetic community of laughter and tears. It's wonderful when God 'sets up' moments of encouragement through friendship.

When my father died, my mother and I were both at his side. Despite the sure warnings from the nursing staff that this was his last day on earth, it still came as a shock when he breathed his last breath. I was still holding his hand when, about ten seconds after his departing, the telephone next to the hospital bed rang. The nurse answered the phone. It was for me. Still holding my father's cooling hand, I took the telephone to my ear. It was my friend Chris, a family doctor who lives in Oregon. He was driving through Canada, and had felt prompted by the Holy Spirit to call me right at that moment. Knowing that I had spent the last few days at the hospital, he had dialled directly, hoping to find me there. He was keen to know why the Lord had inspired him to call at that moment. And as I shared with him how, seconds earlier, my dad had left the earth, he was able to assure me that, despite being thousands of miles away, the love and prayers of his family were with us, in this darkest of moments. As I put down the telephone, I marvelled at a God of kindness who goes to such lengths to 'set up' encouragement. Gideon knew now, beyond a doubt, that victory was assured. Taking time to worship God right there on the battlefield, thankfulness and gratitude surged from his heart as he revelled in the mercy of God. No rushing to battle yet, over-confident and over-eager; rather a moment to return thanks, to celebrate, to reflect and enjoy. The battle could wait; the thanksgiving was important.

※   ※   ※   ※

Wiping sleep from their eyes, the three hundred stirred themselves quickly, fully awakened now by the urgency in Gideon's voice. There was a wildness, an unbridled exhilaration about him as he ran quickly from tent to tent. He was a man fully alive, utterly convinced that God was going to fulfil his promise, that the victory would be theirs. The men were hastily divided into three companies of a hundred, and then the 'weapons' were distributed. They were not so impressive: jars, torches and, of course, trumpets. Their secret weapons were the leftovers of their retreating comrades. If the weaponry was unusual, the battle strategy was incredible. They would station themselves at the edge of the camp. On Gideon's signal, they were to blow the trumpets, shout a war cry, smash the jars, wave their torches and then give another shout. That was it. End of plan.

Never mind the fact that the removal of the jars would reveal the lights of the torches, and thus make their position obvious to the sentries. Forget for a moment the command to yell out, 'A sword for the LORD and for Gideon' when, with a trumpet in one hand and a jar in the other, we can't be absolutely certain that they had swords ...

Think about it. The Midianite camp was huge, so the three hundred would have been stretched rather thinly to surround it, as Scripture suggests. Each man may well have been tens or even hundreds of yards from his nearest fellow soldier. Out there, alone in the night, with the moon lighting up the huge enemy campsite ... what if the plan backfired? What if some lost their nerve, broken by the unbearable tension of the moment, running away in fear? Look at a man standing very still, silently waiting for the word, arm buried deep in the pot where a flaming torch roasted the earthenware. Look at the triumph of trust, as together Gideon's army danced in the dark.

They trusted their leader, choosing to believe that he really had heard from God. In these days when the news so frequently reports the tragedy of the cults, where strong, manipulative leaders have exploited and abused their followers (and sadly, in some 'orthodox' churches too). I also fear the climate of blatant mistrust that seems to exist in some churches. Perhaps the whole concept of leadership has been undermined by preachers who have betrayed the trust of their families and churches by choosing to preach about holiness and sleep with another's partner.

Mistrust of leadership is a powerful thing. The children of Israel were convinced that Moses parted the

waters of the Red Sea only in order to get them out into
the wilderness to kill them (Num. 16:13) – an elaborate
plan if ever there was one! Certainly leaders need to earn
our trust, and those who abuse it deserve the strongest
rebuke and correction, but a measure of trust is vital if
the church is to go forward as a fighting unit under God.

Gideon's army trusted each other. In following this
strange strategy, they placed their lives into each other's
hands. The whole plan depended upon every man playing his part, flowing with the others, shouting together
at the same time. And timing was vital. The moment of
'attack' came at around midnight, at the 'beginning of
the middle watch'. The Midianites had only just posted
new sentries, who would perhaps still be bleary-eyed
from interrupted sleep, their vision not adapted for a
few minutes to the darkness. The analogy is obvious, but
important: dependable people are needed if the church
is to know victory. Battles will not be fought and won by
the careless and the casual who serve only when they
feel like it.

They trusted God as they stood out there in the darkness. The huge encampment must have loomed very
large in the moonlight, but they told themselves: God
will give this massive garrison into our hands. Perhaps
confusion threatened to overwhelm them as they prepared to use their so-called weapons. Who knows how
many questions pressed in on their minds as they peered
through the darkness? But they stood firm, and trusted
anyway.

Could it be that those of us from the evangelical wing
of the church need to develop a closer friendship with
mystery? There are times when we present ourselves as
the people with all the answers, in our catechismic
approach to life. Is someone not healed? Then it must be
because of answer a, b or perhaps c. Is Jesus coming

back? Read this book and then check out this chart. But there are times when there are no answers, and the only thing you can do is to stand and to hold your place, even though it is very, very dark.

❄   ❄   ❄   ❄

John and Cheri Pauls live in Colorado Springs, Colorado. The leaders of a growing church in that city, they and their family have been close friends to my own family over the years. Their home has always been a refuge of love and laughter for me in my frequent travels to that part of the States, with Justin, Jory and Chenille, their three children, always joining in with the fun. Jory had a particular capacity to reduce me to uncontrollable laughter with his dry and astute wit. A keen worshipper and a young man who sensed the call to become a missionary, Jory approached me one day as I walked into the church building to speak at a youth meeting. Feeling rather old, I had donned my trendiest 'Tommy Hilfiger' fleece and black Levis for the event. Jory saw through my ploy and strolled up to me with a broad grin. 'Nice try, Jeff.'

One morning an e-mail from America appeared on my computer screen. With the stark, uncluttered harshness that electronic communication brings, it told of how Jory had been out in the fields, working with his brother, when he decided to go back to the house to pick up some sunglasses and chewing gum. Returning to cross the normally sleepy road, he never saw the truck that ploughed into him and killed him instantly. Kay and I were privileged to be able to fly out to take part in Jory's funeral. Over a thousand people gathered that day to laugh and weep together, in what was one of the most life-changing events that I have ever attended. Travelling there on the plane, I felt such a sense of dread. What words could I say to our friends, so horribly shattered by such a terrible tragedy, the like of which every parent fears? I need not have been afraid. Answers were unnecessary, and to attempt to find some would have been an insult. We laughed and wept together for twenty-four hours, remembering Jory's uniqueness, sensing the pain of his going, celebrating the smile that he was – and is now – on the face of God.

As I watched John, Cheri, Justin and Chenille, smiling through the tears at the funeral, hands lifted towards God, not in anger or doubt but in a wholehearted, determined trust, I saw a sight that must make God weep for joy: that of his people who, through trust, are determined to dance in the dark.

❊   ❊   ❊   ❊

In a second, the still of the night was shattered by the sound of three hundred trumpets, an alarm call that rose up from the edges of the camp. Suddenly the jars were smashed, a strange hollow shattering that filled the still night air. Torches were whipped upright, blazing and tearing at the darkness and a throaty roar rose up in their throats. 'For the LORD and for Gideon . . . a sword for the LORD and for Gideon!' They shouted for their lost children. They shouted for the famine years. They yelled and screamed for the loss of their dignity and hope that had been so ruthlessly crushed by Midian. It was a deafening, colourful, confusing scene, bright light and noise coming from three hundred points on the mountainside at the same time. And the Midianites, so suddenly awakened from sleep, stumbled out of their tents, eyes unaccustomed to the dark and blinded by the lights, and immediately panicked. Perhaps the fearful camels, terrified by the din, stampeded and multiplied the sense of chaos. Surely there were hordes of troops behind the torch-bearers . . . And so, in a bloody fury, imagining that anyone who approached them in the dark might be their enemy, they stabbed and slashed one another in panic. The night was filled with the urgent screams of the dying, as the frantic carnage continued, a self inflicted blood letting. Those who were able grabbed whatever possessions they could, and began to move out eastwards down the valley, towards the River Jordan, their turn to flee now. The sleep was still in their eyes as they hurried away, as fast as possible. And the irony of it all was that there had been no one behind the torch-bearers, no teeming hordes of infantry, no back-up troops, no one at all.

Except God.

❀   ❀   ❀   ❀

Up on one of the slopes, flaming torch still held high in his hand, Gideon stood, eyes wide with wonder. The plan had worked. The hopeless, helpless years were ended. The cursed locusts, the predators, were leaving now. Perhaps the battle screams turned to cheers of joy as the huge Midianite encampment became a teeming mass of activity. They were rounding up the camels as best they could, tents were being abandoned in the desperate rush to get away.

Gideon pondered his next move. He would need to enlist as much help as possible to deal finally with the escaping Midianites. He promptly dispatched messengers into the mountains of Ephraim, inviting the tribe of Ephraim to come down into the lowlands and close off the Midianites' escape route near the Jordan. Some of the original thirty-two thousand men who had been sent on their way in 'the great reduction' were re-enlisted now for the 'mopping up' operation – men from Naphtali, Asher and Manasseh. The battle of Gideon's sword – and the skirmishes that followed it – would claim the lives of around a hundred and twenty thousand enemy swordsmen. The three hundred regrouped, rested and waited while the heralds and messengers were briefed and sent out, and then prepared for the pursuit. The final assault would have to be co-ordinated with the responding men of Ephraim if the trap was to shut tight. The next few days would provide glorious stories of heroism and triumph for countless campfires in years to come. The revolution was in full swing.

Chapter Nine

The Distraction of Criticism

It should have been a moment of loud, colourful celebration: broad smiles, embraces and back-slapping, and the triumphant telling of the battle stories again. Both groups had much to share: Gideon's glorious 'few' had secured their place in history, routing the mighty Midian with a torch and a shout. The men of Ephraim had sealed off the enemy's escape, winning a magnificent victory. It was a moment to be grateful, a time to laugh together. But it was not to be. When the two forces finally met, the Ephraimites were long-faced and cold-eyed. Bitterness simmered and suddenly exploded in white-hot temper. Sharp words were spat out. Fingers jabbed and fists bunched.

Earlier, the men of Ephraim had been quick to respond when the herald arrived and shared his breathless announcement of the victory of the three hundred. But the Ephraimites were both delighted arid angered by the news. They had longed for the day when revenge could be exacted upon their old enemies, the Midianites, and so the story of their flight had thrilled them. But resentment ignited as they pondered the fact that the lad from Ophrah had not consulted them or called them to join in the first skirmish of the war. Why had they not been summoned to Jezreel? Why had no Ephraimite had the privilege of holding a torch high? The Ephraimites were a proud tribe; General Joshua had been from their number. Their city of Shiloh had been home to the tabernacle. Besides, had Gideon of Manasseh forgotten that his tribe had been passed over by Joseph on his deathbed in favour of Ephraim? They had a right to be involved in all-important tribal matters, or so they surmised. They were incensed. But the matter could be dealt with later. It was time to shed some enemy blood.

They began the trek down to the western side of the Jordan, to the waters of Beth Barah, and waited. Soon enough, the first of the fleeing Midianite army appeared, followed by a heaving mass of hurried, frantic escapees, desperate for home. No details are given to us by the writer of Judges concerning the battle strategy of the men of Ephraim, only that they captured two very important prisoners. But elsewhere Scripture throws some light on the massive slaughter that Ephraim engaged in: the psalmist celebrates the death of the two prisoners, Oreb and Zeeb, who were Midianite captains, and describes the slaughter of Midian that day as 'chaff before the wind' (Ps. 83:11-13). Isaiah compares the battle of the rock of Oreb (named after the skirmish) with the slaughter of the Egyptians in the Red Sea – a most noble comparison when you remember the significance of the Exodus in Hebrew thinking.

❋   ❋   ❋   ❋

The two men knew that they had only minutes to live. Blood had stained their own hands since youth; death was no stranger to them, just a dark companion who had been waiting patiently. And now it was friend death's turn. They must have been accomplished warriors, these two. Their names mean 'raven' and 'wolf', and their demise would be the theme of many an Israeli song. The Ephraimites were in the mood for sport, but the numbers of escaping Midianites meant that justice would be meted out swiftly. As the wolf and the raven laughed hysterically, two Ephraimite warriors swung heavy swords again and again and roughly hacked off their heads, bad blood spilt on a good day for Ephraim.

Flushed with their success, the Ephraimites made haste, heading across to the east side of the Jordan to meet Gideon. What was it that motivated the Ephraimites to present the bloody heads of Oreb and Zeeb to him there? Was it truly a moment designed to honour the triumphant Gideon, or were the grim souvenirs passed to him as a thinly-veiled message? Look here, man from Manasseh, we, the men of Ephraim, have fought a successful campaign. Two of the most notorious Midianite leaders have fallen today by our hands . . . From the scalding criticism that followed, the latter interpretation seems more likely to be true.

❄   ❄   ❄   ❄

'Why have you done this to us by not calling us when you went to fight with the Midianites?' The cauldron erupted and overflowed. The faces of the men of Ephraim were contorted with rage, their voices trembling, their words laced with deadly venom.

It must have felt like such a slap in the face for Gideon, who was surely still riding an emotional high following the triumph at Jezreel. Perhaps there is some orchestrated strategy in criticism. It often strikes when we are feeling flushed with success, and so it may help us come down to earth and humility again. But sometimes criticism stabs at the most precious moments of genuine gratitude and thanksgiving. It becomes a robber, snatching joy from us in an instant.

True leaders will often meet criticism. The very nature of leadership is that it brings about change, and so will challenge the resolute defenders of the status quo. But we should not rush to demonise all criticism: it may be God's gift to us, an unwelcome but vital exposure of our blind spots. It may be the difficult service of a faithful friend who loves us too much to allow us to make obvious mistakes. As we will see, even though criticism is always painful, it may be the source of genuine revelation to us; what we want is not always what we need. Sometimes we can be blinded by the strength of our own God-given vision, and become so determined to follow it, that we reject the constructive criticisms of our friends as the attack of the enemy.

But there are also times when, in the moments when we should be celebrating, we are suddenly plundered by the madness of Ephraim.

❋ ❋ ❋ ❋

The Ephraimites were consistent – consistently critical, that is. Later in history, when Jephthah became the prominent judge, they would bring a complaint against him, also at a strategically critical moment of warfare (Judg. 12:1-6). Once again, the Ephraimites protested that they had not been invited to join a battle. Have you ever noticed that critical people sometimes repeatedly get upset about their own pet issues, and can always be relied upon to raise a dissenting voice? They crossed the Jordan and headed in large numbers for Mizpeh, Jephthah's home town but, reluctant to allow his home turf to become a battlefield, Jephthah intercepted them at Zaphon. A fierce argument broke out. Jephthah responded with indignant hostility, insisting that he had indeed issued an invitation.

The assurance did not satisfy the complainers. Ironically, the truth will not satisfy some critics, so determined are they to make trouble whatever the rights or wrongs of their 'cause'. Sometimes the issue that critics present is not really the issue that actually concerns them, which is why solving the presenting issue doesn't always bring peace. There's more, much more, beneath the surface.

Sometimes people criticise because they are deeply unhappy with themselves and attempt to diffuse their own sense of inadequacy by fault-finding. The platform of criticism allows them to feel superior, just for a while, even though they are deceiving themselves: 'Criticism is an attractive option . . . it carries the unspoken implication that we would have done much better than what has been done, without us ever having to demonstrate whether we could or not.'[23]

Thus pride lingers in those self-appointed 'watchmen' and 'watchwomen' who feel that they are on a mission from God to straighten the rest of us out. It takes little skill to diagnose a problem, if no constructive help or cure is to be offered.

The critical Ephraimites were certainly hard-headed and proud, suffering, as they did, with an inflated sense of their own importance. Critics go to great length – and personal effort – to make their point. In order to argue with Jephthah, Ephraim mustered a massive army and crossed the Jordan, expending huge effort (a hike of around thirty miles) and risking inter-tribal war, rather than back down. It would have been so much easier to embrace the high wisdom of humility, and move forward into a joint

---

[23] Tom Marshall, *Understanding Leadership* (Sovereign World, 1991), p. 94

victory. But the operation would be temporarily suspended so that an internal argument could be settled, with the
tragic waste of forty-two thousand Ephraimite soldiers'
lives.

❀　❀　❀　❀

Gideon looked around at the weary faces of the three
hundred, and saw the disappointment enveloping them
like a shroud. Their hearts had soared at the distant sight
of their brothers in arms; now they plummeted into
despair as the words of rejection and accusation flooded
over them, sweeping their joy away. The insanity that
can sweep through a crowd, turning it into a lynch mob
in moments, was igniting in Ephraimite eyes. The complaining became a mass ranting, as men squared up
their shoulders and lifted their chins in proud rage.
Tension crackled, a living thing in the air; brothers had
become adversaries in a moment. They were standing
tiptoe on the precipice of civil war. The mighty victories
would be swept away, as Israel hovered on the brink of
oblivion. Perhaps Gideon raised both arms in the air, a
gesture to beg for quiet, to allow him to speak. The three
hundred stiffened, every nerve taut, adrenaline rushing
through every sinew, seconds from a bloody battle.

Then Gideon's face broke out in a broad smile, his
arms now extended in a gesture of embrace. 'What have
I accomplished compared to you? Aren't the gleanings
of Ephraim's grapes better than the full grape harvest of
Abiezer?'

Silence for seconds that seemed like minutes. Men
catching the eyes of their friends, looking for signals,
seeking to know the mind of the group. And then, very
slowly, warmth grew in eyes that had been cold; faces
creased into smiles. Gideon was humbling himself, playing down his own victory – the grape harvest of Abiezer,

his own clan – against the gleaning of Ephraim's grapes, the triumph over Oreb and Zeeb.

Proverbs declares that 'A gentle answer turns away wrath' (Prov. 15:1). In his considered, thoughtful response, Gideon passed a major test of leadership. Resisting the obvious temptation to be defensive, or arrogant ('Don't you know who I am, or what I've accomplished? How dare you!') Gideon quickly diffused a flash point which could have turned into a war. With just one sentence, there was armistice.

Gideon refused to respond to anger with a like spirit, at least on this occasion. On the contrary, he diffused the situation by meeting accusation with grace; hostility with gentleness. The late Tom Marshall offers some wisdom for those who would aspire to response rather than reaction when faced with criticism

> If it is driven by contention – respond in peaceableness
> If it is driven by malice – respond in love
> If it is driven by meanness – respond in generosity
> If it is driven by pride – respond in humility
> If it is driven by arrogance – respond in teachableness
> If it is driven by deception – respond in truth
> If it driven by mistrust – respond in faith.[24]

Beware the fervency that can come with conviction, or the intensity – or arrogance – that sometimes attaches itself to those who would be holy. Gentleness, a fruit of the work of the Holy Spirit in our lives, should always be present when correction is offered. 'Brothers, if someone is caught in a sin, you who are spiritual should restore him *gently*' (Gal. 6:1, italics mine).

---

[24] Tom Marshall, *Understanding Leadership* (Sovereign World, 1991), p. 98

Leaders should avoid a defensiveness that causes us to reject criticism out of hand because the attitude of the critic is wrong. Sometimes people say the right thing in the wrong way, and we stumble on into error, rejecting the message because of the manner of the messenger. The men of Ephraim were 'sharp', but Gideon still heard them.

Keep prayer high on the list of priorities. I have often wondered if some of those modern-day 'Ephraimites' are actually those who have a genuine gift of insight and perception that has come from God – they see with eyes that the Lord has opened. But a corruption of their gift comes when they refuse to respond appropriately to what they observe. Instead of praying for the lukewarm, they rush to pick up a stick to beat them into commitment. Instead of interceding with the Lord who is building *his* church, the critics begin to act indignantly as if the church belonged to them. When observation and prophetic insight are not used as fuel for prayer and intercession, then strife and conflict are waiting at the door. Or, as one writer put it more simply, 'When we do not pray for one another, we prey on one another.'

Those who would rush to criticism, or make it their hobby, need to hear the sober warning of Jude: 'Certain men . . . have . . . slipped in among you. They are godless men . . . These men are blemishes at your love feasts . . . They are clouds without rain, blown along by the wind; autumn trees, without fruit and uprooted – twice dead. They are wild waves of the sea, foaming up their shame; wandering stars, for whom blackest darkness has been reserved for ever. . . These men are *grumblers and fault-finders* . . .' (Jude 4,12,13,16, italics mine).

The men of Ephraim were appeased, for now, and Gideon was able to get on with the important matter at hand: the defeat of Midian. Unfortunately, as the later and previously mentioned skirmish with Jephthah would prove, the Ephraimites failed to learn from this negative episode in their history. The critical spirit would be their undoing. But then some of us never learn . . .

As for Gideon, he had passed a very important test for now. But our success today guarantees nothing tomorrow. Within a few days, he would face yet more criticism, only this time he would be exhausted, mentally, physically and emotionally. Would he still be able to respond to disappointment and hurt with humility and grace?

❋   ❋   ❋   ❋

The Midianites, most of them back in their home territory now, were probably reeling with a mixture of relief and grief – exhilarated and thankful to have escaped the mysterious force that accompanied the apparently huge army of Israel, and frantic with mourning over the 120,000 of their comrades who had been slain. Their once huge, teeming mass now numbered just fifteen thousand. What a rude awakening: for seven heady years they had strutted and postured as conquerors, and now the mighty oppressors had become the fleeing oppressed. The tables had so suddenly been turned. What, or who, was the force that had transformed the Hebrew cowards into warriors?

They camped and refreshed themselves by the watering holes of Karkor. Satisfied both by the fresh water and the sense that they were safe and secure at last, they didn't even bother to mount a guard. The battle was surely over, and it was time for the whole community to rest and to weep. But they didn't reckon on the tenacity of Gideon. He was on his way, and the faithful three hundred were with him.

❈   ❈   ❈   ❈

The sweat was a salty sheen on his face, trickling into the corners of his eyes, matting his hair into a thick, heavy mass. Every muscle in his body seemed joined in a tired dirge of complaint, screaming for rest and nourishment. Gideon and his few were at the very limits of their endurance; the trek to Karkor demanded a march of one hundred and fifty long miles through arid and difficult terrain. As they plodded on, they knew that the Midianites were a long way ahead – the camels of the enemy and the complaining of Ephraim had ensured that. They kept going, 'faint but pursuing' as the now famous text puts it. Perhaps they were initially driven on by seven long years of pent-up frustration. Perhaps the battle exploits of the sullen Ephraimites stirred them to pursue their own moment of glory. But frustration and aspiration don't fill an empty stomach – they would need to replenish their supplies before the great, final battle. Perhaps the brow of the next hill would reveal a distant city, with the promise of food and drink for the weary warriors. In the meantime, an ocean of sand stretched before them, with a barren horizon in the distance. Gideon looked back over his shoulder for just a moment, anxious for his men. Tiredness and dehydration were creased on to their gaunt faces. Each step now seemed to take impossible effort. They *needed* to find a settlement, an oasis, and they needed to find it quickly. Turning back, he peered out for the thousandth time at the distant horizon, struggling to focus his bloodshot eyes. And then, the sudden outbreak of cheering from behind him, the excitement of those with keener sight, confirmed that he was not imagining things, that this was no mirage. Smoke billowed and puffed its trail up into the blue sky, and as they broke into an impossible run, cheering and shouting like children, other features of the distant settlement became clear. There would be food for aching bellies, and cool water for their parched, sand-specked lips. They were safe.

Succoth was a small settlement on the eastern side of the Jordan, on the dividing line between the Gadite and Manassite territories. It took its name – *Succoth* means 'shelters' or 'tabernacles' – because Jacob had built booths and a dwelling for his family there after he separated from Esau (Gen. 33:17). Excavations have revealed the remains of metal works there – bronze items for Solomon's temple were cast in the area (1 Kgs. 7:46). Gideon would have hoped for a hero's welcome in the town. Living as close as they did to the Midianite heartland, the citizens of Succoth would have taken the brunt of the wrath and oppression of Midian. Now, the liberation force, the freedom fighters, were passing through. Gratitude would surely guarantee a good meal for the victorious band.

It was not to be. Imagine the huge wave of disappointment for Gideon and his men as the terrible truth that they were not welcome washed over them. The leaders of Succoth, anxious not to upset their old Midianite oppressors and neighbours, refused all hospitality. They were hedging their bets, anxious for their own skin, denying their brothers for the sake of self-preservation. What if Gideon and his tiny force were defeated by Midian? If Midian in turn discovered that supplies had been provided by the people of Succoth, then vengeance would be swift and terrible. Their refusal was graphic: 'Are the hands of Zebah and Zalmunna (Midianite princes) already in your hand?' There is a hint here of the Egyptian practice of cutting off the hands of vanquished enemies and holding them as trophies. Whatever the exact meaning, the message from the city officials was clear: Succoth would not help the exhausted task force.

Gideon exploded, and understandably so. He had presided over a supernatural routing of a long-term enemy. He had endured the thankless scolding of the Ephraimites with good grace, and now he had to call his men to stumble on through the desert because of the spineless turncoats of Succoth. Eyes blazing with indignation, he spewed out a torrent of judgement: 'For this cause, when the LORD has delivered Zebah and Zalmunna into my hand, then I will tear your flesh with the thorns and wilderness and with briers . . .'

So, was the fire-and-brimstone-breathing Gideon out of order in threatening the unhelpful and cowardly elders of Succoth with torture? Or was he acting as a righteous judge in Israel, punishing them justly for their crime of passive collaboration with the enemy? Was this genuine justice or the rantings of a man seized by the madness of temper? The commentators are fiercely divided on the issue. Some suggest that Gideon was completely wrong to respond with such ferocious threats: 'Gideon had such great confidence in God that he began to take things into his own hands. Gideon threatened (Succoth) with vengeful words and punished them with exaggerated cruelty. One . . . is left to conclude that Yahweh's Spirit *had left Gideon at this point* . . .'[25] 'It is a personal vendetta which Gideon has been prosecuting so ruthlessly in the Transjordan . . . (earlier) his motivation was obedience to God, but here it is personal revenge . . . how he has changed . . .'[26]

---

[25] E. John Hamlin, *Judges, At Risk in the Promised Land* (Handsel Press, 1991), p. 98, italics mine

[26] Michael Wilcock, *The Message of Judges – the Bible speaks today series* (Leicester: IVP, 1992), p. 86

Others come to the opposite conclusion: 'It is probably correct to see the beating of the elders of Succoth . . .
as a judicial sentence carried out as judge, rather than
indicating a personal vendetta or fit of revenge.'[27] 'The
punishment inflicted by Gideon . . . was well deserved
in all respects, and was righteously executed . . . having
been called by God to be the deliverer and judge of
Israel, it was Gideon's duty to punish the faithless
cities.'[28]

Who really knows whether Gideon was operating in
the anointing or was now on a heady power trip? In his
support, we should remember that he would shortly
strike a powerful blow in battle, routing fifteen thousand with his weary commando force of three hundred.
God was with him still, giving him success. But the presence of God with us to help does not signify divine
approval of everything we do. Grace means that the
Lord often blesses us even though there are glaring areas
of lack in our lives. Gideon would very shortly start to
go beyond the command of God in his life, as the next
chapter will show.

Whatever the truth is, Gideon and his men stomped
out of Succoth, promising to return shortly with victory
and vengeance. They headed east, treading the clinging
sand for four more miles, hoping desperately for a
warmer reception at the golden mounds of Peniel. The
town name meant 'face of God'. It was so named
because it was there that Jacob had wrestled with 'a
Man' until daybreak, and had seen God 'face to face'
(Gen. 32:30). The town boasted a castle, or tower, a land-

---

[27] David Jackman, *Mastering the Old Testament – Judges, Ruth*
(Word, 1993), p. 143

[28] Keil and Delitzsch, *Commentary on the Old Testament vol. 2*
(Hendrickson, 1989), p. 257

mark perhaps visible from a good distance. With weary eyes fixed on that distant spire, the few staggered on. Their hopes were to be cruelly dashed again, because the same frosty response was waiting for them: the tower, which they had hoped was a beckoning beacon of hope and hospitality, was a symbol of arrogance, cowardice and political duplicity. Gideon pronounced solemn judgement as he stood in the tower's shadow: 'When I come back in peace, I will tear down this tower!'

So where did Gideon and his men find their much needed supplies? We are not told. Perhaps we are only told of the churlish people of Succoth and Peniel because of the judgements to come, and other details are unimportant.

Imagine Gideon mustering his men for the final trek to Karkor, a further twenty-five miles' march from Peniel, towards the south-east. Whatever the rights and wrongs of Gideon's judgements, we must concede that he was faithful to the call of God. He faced impossible odds in battle, and still he blew the trumpet and called for the jars to be broken. He met ingratitude and accusation from Ephraim, but he refused to turn back, broken and hurt by the 'friendly fire' of his so-called brothers. Succoth and Peniel closed their doors and turned their backs on him and his hungry men, preferring to play political chess rather than help the conquering heroes. Still Gideon marched on, resolute and determined.

As we conclude this chapter, we should remember that all who would do exploits for God will have to travel by Gideon's route. Consider William Seymour, the black, one-eyed preacher who was used by God in the mighty Azuza Street Revival in Los Angeles in 1906. History has now honoured Seymour as the father of half a billion Pentecostals, an honour he never knew in his lifetime. His is a story of trekking through Succoth.

When he attended a Bible school at Topeka, Kansas, he had to sit outside and listen to the lessons at the classroom window because he was black. When he first began preaching in a storefront chapel in Los Angeles, he was locked out by the congregation – not a promising start. And when the Azuza meetings began, the press launched a violent attack, lampooning the revivalist with mocking cartoons and scaremongering headlines: 'Holy kickers carry on mad orgies . . .' and 'Whites and blacks mix in a religious frenzy . . .' Ironically, the criticisms attracted more and more people, who attended the Azuza meetings just to find out what was going on.

But the cutting words of our brothers wound most deeply, particularly when old friends and even mentors turn against us. Seymour's old Bible school tutor, Charles Fox Parham, a famous Pentecostal pioneer and allegedly a Ku Klux Klan sympathiser, became one of his most vocal and vitriolic critics. Visiting the revival, Parham accused the Azuza people of animism, hypnotism and of having 'familiar spirits and casting spells . . .' Parham wrote: 'Men and women, whites and blacks knelt together or fell across one another – frequently a white woman, perhaps of wealth and culture, could be thrown back into the arms of a buck nigger . . .'

But Seymour just kept going, even though his journey demanded that he tread the irksome pathway through Succoth. Like the pioneers of faith described in the Hebrews Hall of Faith (Heb. 11), Seymour pushed on even though he did not see the fulfilment of the promises of God. The Azuza revival was the result, a legacy many of us share and enjoy today.

Are you passing through Succoth? Forgive my simplistic exhortation, but, whatever else you do, just keep going for God.

Chapter Ten

Surviving Success

Details of the great, final battle are scarce. Passing by Nobah, and the fortified Gadite town of Jogbehah, Gideon and his band inched their way along 'the road of those who dwell in tents', a well-worn caravan route. Probably approaching the Midianites from the north-east, the attack was launched. The Midianites were completely taken by surprise, so convinced were they of their own safety. They had not reckoned on Gideon's tenacity.

Perhaps they were beaten by the psychological devastation of having already lost so many of their comrades. Perhaps they were terrified of the strange, mysterious force they had sensed when the torches had been lit and the jars smashed in unison. The victory was massive and conclusive. The panic-stricken Midianites were at last a spent force. Two very important prisoners were caught as they frantically tried to flee the scene: the infamous Zebah and Zalmunna. Victory was sweet. The very men whose names had been used to taunt the few in Succoth were now Gideon's captives . . .

❈   ❈   ❈   ❈

The young man from Succoth was clearly terrified. Convinced that death was crouching, ready to spring upon him in a second, he shook visibly, his eyes wide with fear. Was torture used to extract the strategic information that Gideon required? Scripture is silent. Perhaps his heart beat faster as he looked across at Zebah and Zalmunna, their hands tied tightly behind their backs. If the two princes were scared, they were giving nothing away. Their eyes were creased in a mocking smile; something was amusing them, even though they were dead men walking. And they *were* amused, albeit by a very private joke. They were the assassins of Mount Tabor. Gideon's two brothers had fallen by their hands. It was ironic that they should be captured by the man from Ophrah. Of course, perhaps Gideon didn't know that they had snuffed the light of life from his brothers as if they were mere animals . . .

The young man risked a look up at the men who were guarding him. Their faces and hands were still smeared with a muddy red. In fact, they seemed to be drenched, blood clogging their fingernails and smearing their forearms. They had danced with death and they were the winners. Out for a stroll in the pass of Heres, enjoying the warm afternoon sun on his back, he had literally wandered into their encampment. What would become of him, now that these men with gore-stained fingers held his life in the balance?

Hand quivering, the unknown and unfortunate youth wrote down a list of Succoth's magistrates and municipal officials. He frantically searched his memory. The instruction was clear: not one should be missed off the list. Seventy-seven names were quickly added.

Scanning the list, Gideon was satisfied. The boy would have no reason to lie, unless he deliberately left off one of his own family from the list of judgement. The

time had come for Judge Gideon to revisit the cities that
had mocked him and his men.

Perhaps there was a hasty gathering in the centre of
the town, summoned urgently when the shouts of the
city lookouts heralded the news. Gideon and his men
were striding resolutely across the sand, and their return
could only mean one thing: they were victors. Midian's
might had been broken. Did the town council huddle
together, desperately searching for ways to atone for
their earlier madness? Did they consider sending out a
peace offering, a gift to hail the conquering hero from
Ophrah, one last desperate attempt to side with the winners? Did they hastily prepare elaborate speeches of
welcome and congratulation, bracing themselves to
smile and bow and scrape and ingratiate their way out
of trouble?

Perhaps the whole town gathered, anxious and fearful, as Gideon strode in, pushing the tethered Zebah and
Zalmunna before them, living trophies triumphantly
displayed. When at last the gathered crowd fell silent as
Gideon shoved the murderous pair into the dust, he
raised his voice for all to hear: 'Here they are! Zebah and
Zalmunna! You taunted me. You said, "Do you already
have their hands in your possession?"'

Then the indictment: 'You said, "Why should we give
bread to your exhausted men?"'

No pronouncement of verdict was needed. They were
guilty as charged. The entire town lowered its eyes in
shame: they had betrayed their nationhood, and their
God. They had sided with the enemy, and the enemy lay
prostrate in the dust before them, princes become slaves.
The list was read with a solemn voice: each man stepped
forward quickly, the desperate cries of his wife and children a sob for mercy. Would the elders of Succoth die
with the princes of Midian? Succoth had been a place of

humiliation for Gideon, where he and his men had been denied the most basic assistance and hospitality. Let Succoth reap what they had sown. Whips of thorns and desert briars – symbols in Scripture of barrenness and wasteland (Is. 7:23 ff.; Lk. 6:44) – were braided. It was a ceremony calculated to humiliate the previously proud officials. The thorns plucked at their skin without mercy, ripping and tearing, cut upon cut, their backs latticed with long, deep gouges brimming with blood. Hysterical wives screamed, a terrible sound. And suddenly it was all over, the gory whips were discarded, bloody fathers clutched their sobbing children, and Gideon and his men, dragging the Midianite princes with them, marched out of the city without another word. It was Peniel's turn, time for them to see the wrathful face of God. The best way to humble them would be to demolish the most obvious symbol of their pride; the famous tower.

Blood begets blood. At Peniel, a terrible battle – or was it a massacre? – ensued. As good as his word, Gideon and his men demolished the proud spire. Did the men of the city put up a fight, a last stand to defend their stronghold? Or were they just marched out to a chillingly methodical execution? Wives became widows, and a city lost its men, its heart and its hope. Once again we ask the question, without a sure answer: was Gideon a man under divine orders or a coward become bully, spinning wildly out of control, his hurt and rejection boiling his heart with bloodlust, a saviour become sadist? As Zebah and Zalmunna heard the cries of the dying, but were themselves spared, pushed once again out of the smoking city of Peniel, they must have wondered: why are we still alive when so many have gone ahead to death?

❋   ❋   ❋   ❋

The execution probably took place back at Ophrah. The victorious local boy, now judge and general, returned to the roaring adulation of friends and family, a litany that drove the weariness of the long march home from his bones. The voices of those who had once called for his death were now raised in the chorus of homecoming welcome: the least in the family had turned out to be the greatest. How they had wondered, thrilled even, at the sight of the tethered princes, the mighty oppressors now fallen. Gideon and the few were the toast of the town, but what was to become of the living spoils of war, Zebah and Zalmunna? A dark rumour began to circulate, whispered behind cupped hands in the town centre, shouted at late-night parties: these two were personally responsible for the deaths of Joash's sons, Gideon's brothers, at Mount Tabor. Had the two been overheard as they whispered about their victory on Tabor? Or had they thrown all discretion to the winds, and taunted their judge and jailer with the news that they had killed his brothers? However it was first birthed, the rumour became a roar, a clamour for justice, and reached Gideon's ears. It was time.

Perhaps the whole settlement gathered for the confrontation between judge and prisoners. The giggling, whispering mass hushed as Gideon raised his hands for silence, and then pointed an accusatory finger at the Midianite two. Sensing that these men were men of honour, men of their word, despite their past savagery, Gideon began the interrogation: 'What kind of men did you kill at Tabor?'

Silence. A crowd not daring to move an inch, not daring to breathe, life and death hanging in the next five seconds. The princes looked Gideon up and down, studying his face carefully, and then one spoke his suicidal confession: 'As you are, so were they . . .' And then, perhaps in a last desperate attempt to flatter their way out of the death that was certain, 'Each one resembled the son of a king . . .'

Gideon's eyes froze. So it was true. These wretches who had become his human prizes, these breathing trophies of war: they were his brothers' killers. How he had wept for his brothers, who had died the death of unwitting victims, denied the martyr's glory of vanquished heroes at war. So it would be fitting for these murderers to die a humiliating death, void of dignity. Not for them an execution at the hands of the new chief-judge of Israel, a death to be sung about around countless Midianite campfires. No, let them die . . . at the hands of a boy. Raped of pride. Objects of laughter and scorn, their blood spilled by little more than a child.

There was no black cap of death. A clinging, eerie silence fell upon the crowd as the sentence was passed. Voice trembling with anger, scarcely controlled, Gideon's eyes bore holes into the two as he spoke: 'They were my brothers, the sons of my mother. As the LORD lives, if you had let them live, I would not have killed you.'

What does it feel like to know that in just a few seconds you will leave this life, this Earth? We all ponder our humanity, and wonder what our last breath will be like: will it be a fight, a struggle for air, before the final blackness? Will we breathe our last in a warm, welcome sleep, body perfectly rested, never to awake? Will our final moment be one of searing, bone-crunching pain, the last noise that we make on earth a scream of agony? When they heard Gideon's words, the two knew that their time had come. Better for it to be over with, quickly now, let blackness, oblivion come.

Dispatch us, Gideon. Play the man and send us to sleep, quickly now.

Eyes widen with horror as Judge Gideon reveals the mode of death. Not a demonic season of torture, to add a verse to their litany. Death by the sword of a boy. Gideon carefully placed his sword into the boy's trembling hands and shouted an excited, high-pitched command: 'Rise, kill them!'

Perhaps Gideon enlisted Jether, his eldest son, as would-be executioner, because he, the judge of all Israel, could not afford to be seen abusing his position, avenging family blood. Perhaps he just wanted the execution to be the final indignity for the two who had stolen Israel's dignity for seven long years. The two closed their eyes, bid light and life and colour goodbye for ever, and braced themselves for the blow. But it was not to be; they would breathe again, a minute-long reprieve. Jether was young, had never seen blood spilled. His hand gripped the sword, but he could find no strength to draw it from its scabbard. Paralysed by fear, he refused to strike. The two, their chests heaving, lungs sucking in final, desperate breaths, lived still, but their eyes were dull and cold as they stared vacantly at Gideon. Weary of waiting for it to be over, one of them quietly made his last request. 'Rise yourself, and kill us, for as a man is, so is his strength . . .'

Ironically, these last words spoken on earth seemed tinged with compassion for young Jether, whose refusal to draw blood risked his own disgrace. Perhaps the Midianite prince almost defends his reluctant executioner, as he declares that the strength to kill does not belong to a boy, but to a man. And almost as soon as the words left his mouth, Gideon whipped out his own sword and brought their lives to a swift end. They fell to the ground, bodies convulsing in the shuddering of death, bubbles of blood bursting at the corners of drooping mouths. Perhaps their legs kicked and jerked as life fled from their limbs, these God-mockers who had coveted the inheritance of Israel.

The psalmist heralds their demise: 'Make . . . all their princes like Zebah and Zalmunna, who said, "Let us take possession of the pasture-lands of God"' (Ps. 83:11).

Then came the moment of truth, the tiny second when perhaps everything changed for Gideon, the pivotal point in his life when he began his long journey, stepping away from and beyond the purposes of God. He looked away from the now lifeless princes, and noticed their camels, stomping, snorting, agitated by the smell of blood. And as the people cheered their good riddances, and serenaded their leader and judge, the sunlight sparkled on the silver and gold ornaments that adorned the camels' necks. Crescent-shaped like moons, these adornments were probably signs of loyalty to an astral cult.

Was Gideon dazzled and seduced by that golden reflection? Speculate with me. Gideon had been sent packing by two cities because they revered the names of the princes more than his humble name. Is it possible that he envied their power and influence? We shall see that Gideon was to set up what looks very similar to a royal household, with concubines and jewels in abundance.

When did the thirst for these trappings first grip his soul?

Did he run greedy eyes over the princes' jewellery collection during the long trek home to Ophrah? How he hated and despised them, these killers of his brothers, but, forced to walk with them through long days in the desert, did he nurse a secret desire to be like them? His own family had known a measure of wealth and influence – his father's position in Ophrah and Gideon's personal collection of servants testified to that. Did Gideon thirst for more?

With the hysterical cheers still ringing out, Gideon walked over to the camels, lifted the precious garlands – the *saharonim* – from their necks. It was easy to justify this act, the taking of booty from a defeated foe. But perhaps something shifted and changed for ever within Gideon as, laden down with silver and gold, he smiled broadly at the adoring, clamouring crowd.

❋   ❋   ❋   ❋

The offer was very attractive. We do not know when it came, and exactly who made the proposal. Scripture records that 'the men of Israel' came to Gideon – probably not all twelve tribes, but more likely only the northern tribes of the western part of the land, whose suffering had been more acute at the hands of the Midianites. The word king – *melek* – is not actually mentioned in the text, but the implication is clear: the people wanted Gideon to rule over them. He could be a warrior prince at last, with a hereditary system of succession to assure his descendants of power. He, and his family, would be set up for life – a very tempting offer for a man who had so recently broken out of obscurity. The offer came from spiritually blind men, who had so quickly forgotten the real source of Gideon's power. '*You* have delivered us from the hand of Midian', they affirmed. Earlier, during his call, Gideon had indeed been commissioned as the saviour of Israel, but he rightly responded to the call of God with a continually repeated declaration of dependence: *God* would save Israel, by *Gideon's* hand. The Lord was the power, his servant was merely the instrument. At the selection of the three hundred, God affirmed that he truly was the source, working through Gideon's tiny, divinely depleted army (Judg. 7:7). Now, Gideon was being elevated as sole saviour, the crown of Israel seized from Yahweh's head, and offered for a bastard coronation.

To his credit, Gideon refused the offer, protesting that God and God alone would rule his people. But sometimes pious words disguise a divided heart. Our speculation is ended here. It is absolutely certain that Gideon's next decision was disastrous. A moment of compromise can usher in the destruction of a lifetime's work. Gideon asked for an offering – for himself – a lion's share of the plunder seized in battle. When did God ever command him to do such a thing? We don't know whether it was the seductive glitter of the gold, or the intoxicating atmosphere of adulation and popularity, that caused Gideon to take leave of his senses. But before we rush to condemn him outright, we should remember that Satan will either try to hinder us from obeying God, or will push us to go beyond what God has asked of us. A garment was spread out, and dutifully each man stepped forward and threw the golden earrings onto it. When the huge bounty was counted up, it was a king's ransom: seventeen hundred shekels (about fifty pounds of gold). One writer estimates that Gideon collected around five thousand gold rings – or even more – that day. The men of Israel had also acquired a massive collection of crescent ornaments (little moons) and pendants (pear-shaped ear drops). Then there were neckbands that had circled the necks of countless camels, and the fine purple robes, once the pride of princes, were passed to him as well. He has refused the offer of kingship, but now he has a king's treasury and a king's wardrobe. He will develop a king's harem. His sons will live like royal princes, stirring in them, tragically, a desire to continue their 'royal' lifestyle. And – one of the most tragic of all his decisions – he will have a son by one of his concubines, and will name him Abimelech, a name which means 'my father is the king'.

But this was not the worst of it. The final downfall came with Gideon's 'bright' idea to make an ephod, a priestly vestment.

❊   ❊   ❊   ❊

The ephod was not an image of Yahweh, or an idol, as some scholars have maintained. Rather it was the construction of the shoulder-dress of the high priest. The ephod was a finely crafted apron, covering both the front and back of the wearer with the 'Urim and Thummim' set into it. These stones were used by the priest to discover the will and mind of God: 'It has been suggested that the Urim and Thummim were two flat objects; one side of each was called "Urim", "to curse", and when both displayed this side the answer was negative; the other side was "Thummim", "to be perfect", and a complete Thummim meant "yes"; one Urim and one Thummim meant "no reply".'[29]

Perhaps the idea seemed logical – some of the most fiendish ideas do. For a start, the rightful high priest at Shiloh – whoever he was – was not functioning well. There is no mention of him being consulted, or the use of Urim and Thummim in the Gideon story. Secondly, Gideon had made an offering, a priestly act, at the winepress. He had offered a sacrificial bull on the rebuilt Yahweh altar at Ophrah, and he had a good track record of inquiring and indeed hearing from God, particularly before battle, a time when priests heard from God concerning the outcome of war. An ephod of consultation

---

[29] H. H. Rowley, *The Faith of Israel*, quoted in the *New Bible Dictionary* (Leicester: IVP), p. 1306

would be 'convenient' for Gideon and his family. So
what was so wrong?

Three problems appear. First, it seemed that Gideon
stepped out of his calling in his 'self-consecration as a
priest'[31] Once again, as when the original offering of gold
was taken, he was doing what God had not asked him to
do, and all in the name of a good idea. God had called
Gideon as general and judge, not as priest. Moses struck
the rock twice, and stepped beyond his call (Num. 20:
11). The disciples James and John, inebriated by supernatural power, offered to call down fiery judgement on
a Samaritan village (Lk. 9:54), and Jesus rebuked them,
as he did Peter, who in his own way tried to thwart the
divine plan (Mt. 16:23). William Branham, controversial
man of miracles, longed to be a Bible teacher, and
allegedly entangled himself in heresy. George Jeffreys,
the Welsh Pentecostal pioneer who blazed a trail for God
seventy years ago, stepped beyond his calling as a
revivalist and evangelist and tried to become a denomi-
national reformer. His biographer laments the step: 'As
a revivalist, he was without equal. As a reformer, he was
a disaster . . .'[30]

Secondly, perhaps Gideon made this terminal error
because he was trying to make permanent an arrangement that was designed by God to be temporary. Gideon
had been called by God to build altars and hear
directives, during the period of his mission. Now the
mission was over, and Gideon wanted the arrangement
to continue. How many initiatives, programmes and
movements have been genuinely birthed by the inspira-
tion of God's Spirit, yet continue long after their period

---

[30] Desmond Cartwright, *The Great Evangelists: the Remarkable
Lives of George and Stephen Jeffreys* (Marshall Pickering),
p. 144

of anointing or usefulness, institutional monuments to what used to be? Perhaps it was misguided nostalgia that provoked the Israelites to eventually 'worship' the ephod, which was displayed at Ophrah. When good things that God has birthed become ponderous institutions and subtle obstacles to his purposes, are they not idols in disguise?

Why did Gideon try to perpetuate the arrangement of revelation and direction with the construction of a do-it-yourself ephod? Was there within Gideon a hankering for signs and heaven-sent messages that bordered on addiction? Our strengths can so easily become our weaknesses. Gideon's strength was that he was able to hear from God. Gideon's weakness was that he *had* to hear from God, hence the less than ideal arrangement with the fleece. God responded kindly, but there was still a deep, unresolved insecurity within Gideon that demanded that he keep on hearing.

Others have suggested that Gideon deliberately diverted the focus of worship away from the central sanctuary at Shiloh, because that city was sited in Ephraimite territory. Old wounds can run deep, though this suggestion of a deeper political motive is in no way substantiated.

Whatever the reasons for the development of the ephod, the result was horrendous, with one of the strongest statements of the entire book of Judges: '. . . Israel *prostituted themselves* by worshipping it there . . .'

The prerogative of the Aaronic priesthood had been unwittingly invaded by Gideon's action. The ephod distracted the people away from the central shrine of Shiloh, fragmenting the core of their religion and setting them up to drift eventually back into Baalism. It is tragic that the man with the blazing eyes who smashed up his father's Baal altar was now setting in place the mechanism that would cause the old Baal altars to be erected once more. 'The Lord intended to preserve the one geographical focus of worship at the "tent of meeting", rather than allowing numerous shrines and, with them, local cults and deities . . .'[31]

*   *   *   *

Did Gideon know that the end was not as glorious as the beginning, as he lived out his last years in fine style at Ophrah? Much *had* been achieved through the ordinary little man from the winepress: the mighty arm of Midian had been broken, and a forty-year period of peace had begun, which was no mean feat. Gideon most likely continued to serve the nation as judge during this time. Considering the fact that they had offered him the kingship, it seems unthinkable to suggest that he just disappeared from public life and ministry. His presence was certainly a restraining influence on the people. It was his death that signalled their wholesale return to Baalism. Turn that tragic fact around and we see that, as long as he was alive, Gideon continued to maintain a high level of positive input. The latter years were 'good' for Gideon in material terms, if prosperity is deemed always to be good. He lived the high life, with numerous wives and offspring. And he lived 'to a good old age'.

But look beyond the surface, past the glitter and the trappings of power and prestige. The land is quiet, the judge is at Ophrah, but the seeds of prostitution have been quietly sown into the very heart of Israel. The decay would become tragically evident when Gideon died: Israel would effectively spit on his memory, turn-

---

[31] David Jackman, *Mastering the Old Testament – Judges, Ruth* (Word, 1993), p. 146

ing once again from God and even going so far as to set up a shrine to Baal-Berith at Shechem. And then Gideon had nurtured a son with a despotic and demonic ambition. Abimelech, 'my father is the king', is just waiting for his father to die, and then he will make a bloody claim for the right to rule.

Urged on by his mother, Abimelech was to massacre sixty-nine of his brothers – all of Gideon's sons except Jotham – in one day's work at Ophrah. A thousand men and women were to be burned to death in the tower of Shechem (Judg. 9:49). Abimelech himself was destined to die at the hand of his armour-bearer while attacking another tower, once again to burn its inhabitants alive. A woman inside the tower dropped a millstone on his head, crushing his skull. Terrified more of the thought of being dispatched by a woman than by death itself, he commanded his faithful armour-bearer to run him through. Just as the two Midianite princes had begged for Gideon to end their lives, so Abimelech, the self-appointed prince, would go to his grave in the same manner.

Gideon would not see all of this; he died a peaceful death at Ophrah, where they laid him in his father's grave. His was a lifetime of mostly good, but he left behind a bitter legacy. After all the potential, the hope, the opportunity to dance in covenant with the faithful God, Gideon left a somewhat barren inheritance. He had walked with the God who still calls us to bear good fruit, fruit that will last, as we live in him (Jn. 15:1-5). He had done some mighty exploits but, in his later choices and decisions, he had somewhat drifted away from the One who makes it plain for us all: 'Without me, you can do nothing' (Jn. 15:5). His was a life that personifies this simple truth; when we stay close to God, rich, wonderful, luscious fruit grows. When we drift away from him, the nettles and brambles begin to appear.

Gideon gave the elders of Succoth the whip of braided thorns and briars. Gideon's loins gave Israel a ruler who would be prophetically denounced by his brother Jotham as a 'bramble' king, a living whip for their backs:

'Finally all the trees said to the thornbush, "Come and be our king." The thornbush said to the trees, "If you really want to anoint me king over you, come and take refuge in my shade . . ."'(Judg. 9:14,15).

When our history-making is ended, and the Good Judge weighs up *our* lives, what will our legacy be: the fruit of abiding faithfulness, or a crop of thistles? Our daily choices determine the answer; choose well and as we bid Gideon goodbye, let's hear the call to break out of the winepress. Let heroism creep into your Monday mornings. Confront the modern altars of Baal. And never forget the key, the vital truth that makes the difference between fruit and thorns, power and weakness: the Lord is with *you*, mighty warrior.

£2.99 ISBN: 1-85078-499-X

If you have enjoyed reading through this book, you may like to study more on Gideon's life and how to put the principles he learned into practice. Elizabeth McQuoid's workbook, *Gideon – Losing to Win* is available from Spring Harvest Publishing, suitable for individual or small group use.

The workbook looks closely at the life of Gideon and how his battles can be our battles too. We face issues such as wanting to have a closer encounter with God, how to make a stand and when, becoming more like Jesus – how can we help the process along?, what plan does God have for our lives, can we miss it and how do we keep our focus sharp? All these topics are covered in the workbook, which is easy to use, challenging and informative.

Spring Harvest workbooks are available from your local Christian bookshop or directly from Spring Harvest on 01825 769000 or at www.springharvest.org.

Other titles in the Bible character workbook series look at Moses, David, Esther and Ruth.

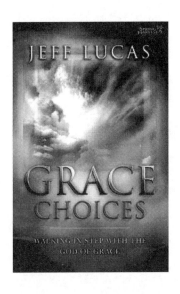

Grace Choices
£7.99 ISBN 1-85078-554-6

In this powerful book, Jeff Lucas unpacks grace in its fullness and shows how, if you choose, grace can work through you and in you to transform your relationships, your church and your life. With his trademark mixture of insight, humour and passion, this book will show you how to take the grace God offers you as you choose to change your world.

'Jeff Lucas is an absolute gift to the church... a brilliant, witty and challenging book.'
Andy Hawthorne, Director of The Message Trust

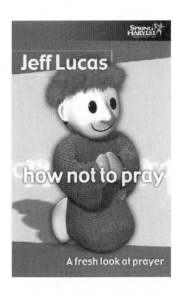

How not to Pray
£7.99 ISBN 1-85078-452-3

No one should be allowed to be so hysterically funny, insightful and transparently challenging and get away with it! You will laugh and then want to pray.
Joel Edwards, General Director, Evangelical Alliance (UK)

A liberating, humorous, down-to-earth, up-to-heaven approach, not just to the activity of prayer but how to live a prayerful, Christ-connected life.
Mark Greene, London Institute for Contemporary Christianity